National Gallery Technical Bulletin

Volume 17, 1996

National Gallery Publications, London

Distributed by Yale University Press

Series Editor: Ashok Roy

First published in Great Britain in 1996 by
National Gallery Publications Limited
5/6 Pall Mall East, London SW1Y 5BA

British Library Cataloguing-in-Publication Data
A catalogue record for this journal is available
from the British Library

ISBN 1 85709 113 2
ISSN 0140 7430

Edited by Diana Davies and Jan Green

Page layout & origination by
Goodfellow & Egan Ltd, Cambridge

Printed in Great Britain by Balding + Mansell, Peterborough

Front cover: Giampietrino, *Salome*; detail of Plate 1, page 4.

Supported by

GlaxoWellcome

Contents

Plate 1 Giampietrino, *Salome* (NG 3930), *c*.1510–30. Poplar, 68.6 × 57.2 cm.

Giampietrino, Boltraffio, and the Influence of Leonardo

LARRY KEITH AND ASHOK ROY

Leonardo da Vinci's activity in Milan, datable in two periods from 1482 to 1499 and from 1507 to 1512/13, saw the production of some of his most important paintings, including the National Gallery's own *Virgin of the Rocks* (Fig.1).[1] It was also notable for the emergence of a group of Milanese painters that adopted his manner, whether in appropriating his compositional motifs or in responding to his extraordinary painterly effects. These artists are well represented in the National Gallery, and even a superficial survey of works by Boltraffio, Bramantino, Cesare da Sesto, Giampietrino, Luini, Marco d'Oggiono, Martino Piazza, de Predis and Solario in the Collection shows something of the extent and variety of Leonardo's influence in Milan. The recent cleaning and restoration of National Gallery pictures by two of these artists – Giampietrino's *Christ carrying his Cross* (Plate 2) and his *Salome* (Plate 1), and Boltraffio's *Virgin and Child* (Plate 3 and Fig. 10)[2] – has allowed the opportunity to examine closely their materials and technique, and, by extension, to consider more fully the nature and degree of their debt to Leonardo.

While a general scholarly consensus has emerged concerning Giampietrino's oeuvre, only one picture is dated, there are no signed works, and therefore all of his works are assigned attributions.[3] Little is known about his life and the very use of the name Giampietrino is conjectural, it having been applied to this group of pictures as a result of its appearance in Leonardo's *Codex Atlanticus* in a list of other painter/pupils.[4] A tradition dating back to Lomazzo has tied this reference to a 'Pietro Rizzo' or 'Pietro Riccio milanese pittore, discepolo di Leonardo da Vinci'.[5] Recent scholarship has shown Lomazzo's (Giovanni) Pietro Rizzi

to have been active significantly earlier (documented between 1481 and 1493) than the body of work now given to Giampietrino, whose single known dated work is from 1521.[6] While Lomazzo's identification of Leonardo's 'Giampietro' in his treatise, itself written between 1497 and 1500, may be correct, recent archival research has linked the pictures now known as Giampietrino with yet another painter, Giovanni Pietro Rizzoli, who seems to have been active until around 1540.[7]

Plate 2 Giampietrino, *Christ carrying his Cross* (NG 3097), *c*.1510-30. Poplar, 59.7 × 47 cm.

5

Fig. 1 Leonardo da Vinci, *The Virgin of the Rocks* (*The Virgin with the Infant Saint John adoring the Infant Christ accompanied by an Angel*) (NG 1093), *c*.1508. Wood, 189.5 × 120 cm.

Plate 3 Giovanni Antonio Boltraffio, *The Virgin and Child* (NG 728), *c*.1493–9. Walnut, 92.7 × 67.3 cm. Detail.

However designated, the paintings traditionally ascribed to Giampietrino[8] do form a stylistically individual and coherent whole. His main stylistic influences seem to have been Marco d'Oggiono, Cesare da Sesto and, above all, Leonardo. His several large altarpieces have recently been given a relative chronology based on a perceived stylistic evolution,[9] but also typical of the artist (and much more difficult to date) is the production of small-format half-length representations of classical or biblical subjects, often executed in multiple versions with varying degrees of studio participation and considerable variation in quality.[10] Both the *Salome* and *Christ carrying his Cross* fall into this latter category, and significantly both have compositions that are clearly derived from Leonardesque prototypes.

A silver-point study of *Christ carrying his Cross* by Leonardo now in Venice (Fig. 2) is clearly the compositional source of the National Gallery Giampietrino.[11] Generally dated between 1497 and 1500, it and other preparatory drawings may have been studies for a painting by Leonardo which has been lost or, perhaps no less likely, for a painting executed by a pupil or associate. Giampietrino's picture is one of many by a variety of artists active in and around Lombardy which reflect this composition.[12]

The National Gallery panel is one of several more or less replica versions of the subject by Giampietrino,[13] suggesting the repeated use of the same studio cartoon. Infra-red reflectography clearly shows the traces of the cartoon transfer[14] in the National Gallery version (Figs. 3a and 3b), particularly visibly delineating the contours of the brow, eyes, and nostril. Another version now in Budapest (Fig. 4), shows similar traces of cartoon transfer (Figs. 5a and 5b); the use of the same cartoon for both pictures was proved beyond reasonable doubt by the exact coincidence of a tracing of the London picture laid on to the Budapest panel.[15]

Infra-red examination of two Giampietrino paintings now in the Brera, *The Magdalen seated in Prayer* (Plate 4) and *The Magdalen*, both show traces of the *spolvero* technique of cartoon transfer, where charcoal is rubbed through holes pricked along the contours of the drawn cartoon.[16] The fact that other versions exist of each of these pictures is further

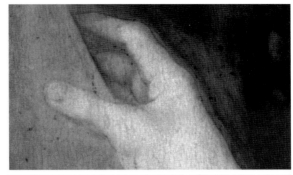

Fig. 2 Leonardo da Vinci, *Christ carrying his Cross*, 1497–1500. Silver-point on grey prepared paper, 11.6 × 9.1 cm. Venice, Galleria dell'Accademia.

Figs. 3a and 3b Giampietrino, *Christ carrying his Cross* (NG 3097). Infra-red reflectogram details showing the traces of cartoon transfer. The use of carbon-containing black pigment in the *imprimitura* paint mixture has somewhat reduced the contrast between the black used in the underdrawing and the white gesso ground.

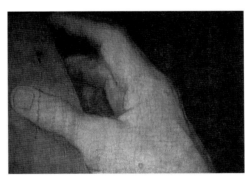

Fig. 4 Giampietrino, *Christ carrying his Cross*. Wood, 62 × 49 cm. Budapest, Szépmüvészeti Múzeum.

Figs. 5a and 5b Giampietrino, *Christ carrying his Cross*. Budapest, Szépmüvészeti Múzeum. Infra-red reflectogram details showing the traces of cartoon transfer.

Plate 4 Giampietrino, *The Magdalen seated in Prayer*. Wood, 60 × 50 cm. Milan, Brera.

indication of the level of production and common reuse of cartoons in the workshop.[17]

The composition of the *Salome* is also derived ultimately from another Leonardo composition, a lost *Leda and the Swan*, here shown in a contemporary copy by another Milanese artist close to Leonardo, Cesare da Sesto (Fig. 6). Numerous studies from Leonardo's hand have survived which emphasise the indebtedness of Giampietrino to Leonardo's composition, such as the study for the *Head of Leda* from the Royal Collection (Fig. 8).[18] In the *Salome* the *contrapposto* twist of the head, torso and outstretched arm is clearly based on the Leonardo prototype; this borrowing is more clearly visible in another related Giampietrino composition, the *Suicide of Cleopatra* (Fig. 7) in the Louvre, Paris, in which the figure is unclothed but otherwise virtually identical to Salome. The underdrawing of the *Salome* was executed in brown paint containing no carbon and hence undetectable by infra-red examination,[19] but the same cartoon was evidently used for both it and the *Cleopatra*. A superimposition of the *Salome*

and the *Cleopatra* in false colour (Plate 5), adjusted to scale, shows the figures to be almost exactly aligned, with only minor adjustment of the outstretched arm. Remarkably, the hand of Cleopatra that holds the asp has been shifted slightly and given to the executioner in the *Salome*. Clearly the cartoon has been reused, and it is not difficult to imagine the elaborately bunched drapery around Salome's shoulder and sleeve or the head of the Baptist as the subjects of separately drawn studies, modified and added to the basic cartoon composition. Such a study from Giampietrino does exist for the head of the Madonna in the altarpiece, dated 1521, for San Marino a Pavia, now in the Fitzwilliam Museum, Cambridge (Fig. 9). In fact the rather less convincingly constructed figure of the executioner is perhaps due to his being not entirely successfully fitted into a pre-existing composition.

Yet Giampietrino's interest in and borrowings from Leonardo are not restricted to matters of composition alone, but also include other aspects of painting technique. The strong *chiaroscuro*

8

and dark backgrounds of Giampietrino's small-format panels are clearly an attempt to emulate the more striking pictorial effects that Leonardo had introduced to Milan.[20] However, it is not certain how much direct contact Giampietrino would have had with Leonardo's actual painting methods and it would be misleading to assume that the imitation of Leonardo's effects required direct reproduction of his techniques. Examination and analysis of the National Gallery Giampietrino panels demonstrate this distinction.

Christ carrying his Cross and *Salome* have standard supports for this period: both are on panels identified as poplar[21] and have white gesso grounds bound in glue. The visual effect of the pure white of the gesso is diminished by the application of stiffly brushed, rather opaque *imprimiture* of a light brownish grey in the case of the *Christ*[22] and of a similar warm mid-grey for the *Salome*. The ridged texture of the underlayer is visible through the surface paint and the brushstrokes are unrelated to compositional form. This *imprimitura* is visible in many areas of Christ's flesh, for example on the chin above the jawline, around the eye-socket (Plate 6) and in the middle tones of the lower torso. In the *Salome* the underlayer is also visible as a warm tone, particularly in the half shadows of her hand and forearm, the Baptist's left cheek and temple, and much of the executioner's flesh. It is particularly evident in his white sleeve. The use of these *imprimiture* presumably played a key role in the intended tonal modelling; however, both greater transparency and local wearing of the paint layers on top have increased their visual effect beyond that intended by the painter.

This underlayer was not a part of the optical build-up of the draperies, even within the different techniques employed in the two pictures. In *Christ carrying his Cross* the deep red drapery is remarkable for the manner of its construction: beneath dark red lake glazes lies an unusual strongly coloured dense red-brown underpaint consisting of vermilion, red earth and black, with an increased proportion of black used under the shadows of the folds.[23] The overall effect is restrained in spite of the intensity of colour and creates a more naturalistic chromatic effect. Some fading of the upper red glaze, the extent of which can be assessed

Fig. 6 Cesare da Sesto, *Leda and the Swan*. Wood, 96.5 × 73.6 cm. From the collection of the Earl of Pembroke, Wilton House.

Fig. 7 Giampietrino, *The Suicide of Cleopatra*. Wood, 73 × 57 cm. Paris, Musée du Louvre. © Photo R.M.N.

9

Plate 5 Superimposed image of Giampietrino's *Salome* and *Cleopatra*. Digital images of the two panels have been rescaled so that they have the same resolution (in pixels per millimetre) with respect to the original paintings. The monochrome images of *Salome* and *Cleopatra* have been assigned to the red and green channels respectively in this superimposed image. The yellow areas show where the two compositions align, suggesting the use of the same cartoon as the basic compositional tool.

Fig. 8 Leonardo da Vinci, *Head of Leda*, detail. Pen and ink over black chalk on paper, 19.8 × 16.6 cm (irregular). Windsor, Royal Collection: Leoni volume (12516). Detail of the principal study from the sheet.

from protected paint at the edge of the picture, has not significantly affected the carefully considered intensity of the drapery colour. A similar layer structure, although with less black pigment, occurs in the darker parts of Salome's red dress (Plate 7) (in the skirt and the lower sleeve of the far arm). In contrast, the elaborate drapery of the near sleeve and bodice makes use of a more conventional system of modelling, with a red glaze over a light pink underpaint of white mixed with red lake. Here, fading is more extensive and more distorting.

The modelling of the flesh relies on fairly straightforward methods. In the *Christ*, the basic structure is worked as a single layer of light-coloured paint, varying in thickness and as a result also in tone; this handling is particularly clear around the eye-socket and across the bridge of the nose, where the thinner paint is modified by the warmer colour of the underlying *imprimitura* (see Plate 6). In Giampietrino's modelling of flesh, the final stage in the production of the illusion of relief was characteristically achieved by the application of dark translucent glazes to create the deepest shadows and their transitions. These glazes were used to depict the strongest shadows in the eye-socket, forearm and torso. The range of contrast in modelling was restricted by the application of a final, extremely thin overall toning layer consisting of warm dark pigments and black in a medium essentially of walnut oil, with a little resin. This unusual pigmented glaze layer is contemporary with the rest of the paint; it cannot be seen in any of the craquelure network and in cross-section is applied directly on to the lower paint layers, with no intervening varnish. Although applied to the entire picture, it is most important in its effect on the lighter values of the flesh, which appear selectively muted (see Plate 8).[24]

In the *Salome*, examination of the method of flesh painting reveals an additional stage in its build-up: forms summarily transferred from the cartoon are worked up and modelled in thin, fluid translucent dark brown paint over the *imprimitura*. The basic *chiaroscuro* created in this preliminary working is retained in the final modelling – not in the deepest shadows, but as the visible underlayer for the thinly scumbled transitional half-tones and lighter valued shadows. This scumbled undermodelling is distinguishable from the more conventionally glazed shadows by its characteristically cooler tonality, which is an optical effect of thin light-coloured paint applied over dark. This technique provides a luminous quality unattainable with glazing of dark over light and is particularly successful in creating more subtle, sculptural modelling. The effect is seen most clearly in the triangular shadow at the base of Salome's throat in the transition between highlight and shadow at the line of her jaw. The same technique is evident in the left eye-socket of the Baptist and the executioner's cheekbone. The darker and warmer shadows were then created by final glazing, as in the *Christ*.

Some idea of the basis of these techniques for painting flesh can be gauged from the unfinished *Head of a Young Girl* in Parma (Plate 9), which is attributed to Leonardo.[25] In this *abbozzo*, on poplar panel, it is possible to see how Leonardo develops light and shade in the construction of flesh, particularly illustrating the importance of the dark undermodelling in the scumbled half-shadows. Giampietrino's method in the *Salome* seems close to this practice.

However, to assess properly the relationship of these works to Leonardo's technique, account must be taken of changes in condition, most fundamental of which are the colour changes that have occurred in Giampietrino's paint layers. In the *Christ* these are most significant in the appearance of the flesh paint, where red lake has faded, resulting in a greyer skin tone than had been depicted originally. We have noted above that some loss of colour of the red glaze on the drapery is less distorting.

Changes in materials have affected the appearance of the *Salome* even more fundamentally. This is largely the result of a more ambitious composition, where a greater number of figures required a broader range of colour and tone to provide the desired overall balance, local variety and directed lighting. The present dominance of red, pink and brown tones would have been complemented by the colour of the stripes on the tablecloth; these are now a deep rust colour but were originally a strong, saturated, rich green, worked in a 'copper resinate' glaze. The degree of this change, and the implications for the overall compositional balance, can be judged from the extreme lower edge where something of the original

colour remains unaltered (Plate 10). A similar transformation, of lesser compositional significance, has occurred in the copper-containing glazes of the executioner's collar and hat, laid over dark orange-brown paint, which would have created an olive-brown colour. As these glazes are underpainted with darker tones than those used in the tablecloth, the effect of their colour change is considerably less important for the reading of the picture. The red colours themselves have shifted as well; as we have noted above, the fading of the red lake in Salome's dress is now particularly evident where it has occurred over a lighter underpaint, which gives undue prominence to the light underlayer. The actual degree of fading is also probably greater as a result of light being reflected rather than absorbed by the underpaint, in effect giving the overlying glaze a double exposure of light.[26] This localised fading has misleadingly increased the tonal contrast between the near and far sides of the dress; at

Fig. 9 Giampietrino, *Head of the Madonna* (study for the altarpiece of San Marino a Pavia, 1521). Red and black chalk on red prepared paper, 23.4 × 16.9 cm. Cambridge, Fitzwilliam Museum.

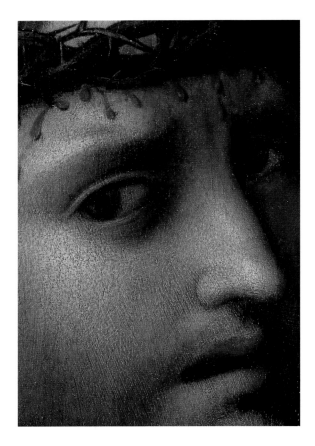

Plate 6 Giampietrino, *Christ carrying his Cross* (NG 3097). Detail showing the warmer tone of the underlying *imprimitura* visible in the transitions around the eye-socket; the deepest shadows are created with darker translucent glazes.

the same time it has diminished the colour intensity by comparison with the unfaded part that can be seen along the bottom edge, where it has been protected by the frame rebate (see Plate 1). In comparison, the underpaint of the red drapery in *Christ carrying his Cross* and in the darker parts of Salome's dress, while now more visible, was of a roughly similar tone to the subsequent glaze.

Fading of red lake pigment has also altered the appearance of Salome's flesh. While some colour remains in parts of the face, Salome's complexion is unnaturally pale and is likely to have been generally considerably more pink. This can be deduced from the presence of red lake pigment in the flesh mixtures which is detectable in cross-section, particularly in UV light;[27] the lake, although not applied as a glaze, has faded within the light-coloured flesh paint matrix. Also, a semi-transparent undergarment passing over the shoulders and across the breast was originally depicted largely as a relative absence of colour in flesh shown beneath it; the faded uncovered flesh, originally rosier, is now virtually indistinguishable from its veiled counterpart.[28] The diaphanous quality of this undergarment is now only clearly visible where it passes over the far shoulder, which is darker, and where it continues down over the arms, particularly at the cuff around the wrist. A similar distinction in flesh tone can also be

Plate 7 Giampietrino, *Salome* (NG 3930). Cross-section of deep plum-coloured shadow from the skirt of Salome's dress showing red lake glaze over a red-brown underpaint of red earth mixed with black. A fragment of gesso and the dense, warm grey *imprimitura*, containing lead white and a little brownish black, are present beneath. Original magnification 650 ×; actual magnification 540 ×.

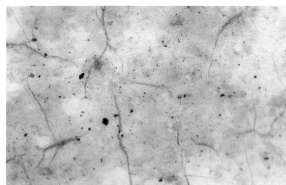

Plate 8 Giampietrino, *Christ carrying his Cross* (NG 3097). Photomicrograph of the shadow of Christ's finger taken directly on the picture surface under the compound microscope in reflected light at 250 ×. The final thin brown toning (pigmented) glaze applied over the entire picture surface, which exerts an optical effect most strongly in the light passages (particularly in the flesh paint), is visible over the pale coloured underlayer. Actual magnification 220 ×.

assumed to have been present originally between the arm and wrist. This change in Salome's complexion, which now appears virtually undistinguishable from that of the Baptist, has eliminated one of the painter's key conceits: a demonstration of the contrasts between the swarthy executioner, the delicate blush of Salome, and the deathly pallor of the Baptist.[29]

Rich, decorative local colour was an important constituent of Giampietrino's style, and its use is instructive for what it reveals about his *leonardismo*. In Leonardo's paintings an overall pictorial unity produced by a tightly controlled, restricted range of tone and value was a central feature. The sculpture-rivalling relief of the National Gallery's cartoon of the *Virgin and Child with Saint Anne and Saint John the Baptist* (NG 6337), with its severely restricted palette, illustrates Leonardo's primary concern with the creation of depth through the manipulation of value, not colour. In painting, while he did develop techniques of exploiting colour of diminishing intensity to create aerial perspective, the intrinsic beauty of certain naturally high-key pigments was as a rule deliberately and consistently subordinated to the constraints of his greater tonal discipline.[30] Leonardo's late *Saint John the Baptist* in the Louvre stands as a clear example of an extremely limited palette achieving an extraordinary sculptural presence. Although Giampietrino may have attempted to create this effect with devices like the toning layer on the *Christ carrying his Cross*, his use of colour was in general more decorative. Even in its ruined state, enough of an impression of Leonardo's mural of *The Last Supper* remains to underscore differences in palette with the more highly saturated local colour of Giampietrino's well-known copy in the Royal Academy, London.[31]

An artist capable of a more subtle understanding of Leonardo was Giovanni Antonio Boltraffio (1467–1516), who was working in Leonardo's studio by 1491[32] and independently by 1498.[33] Vasari also mentions Boltraffio studying with Leonardo, and describes and dates the so-called 'Casio Altarpiece', now in the Louvre, to 1500.[34] Two other works are documented: a *Saint Barbara* of 1502 in Berlin (Staatliche Museum) and the 1508 'Lodi

Plate 9 Leonardo (attributed), *Head of a Young Girl* (*La Scapiliata*). Poplar, 24.6 × 21 cm. Parma, Museo Nazionale.

Plate 10 Giampietrino, *Salome* (NG 3930). Detail from the bottom right edge showing protected and relatively unaltered 'copper resinate' green glaze on the tablecloth stripes.

13

Fig. 10 Boltraffio, *The Virgin and Child* (NG 728), 1493–9. Walnut, 92.7 × 67.3 cm.

Fig. 11 Boltraffio, *The Virgin and Child*. Wood, 83 × 63.5 cm. Budapest, Szépmüvészeti Múzeum.

Altarpiece' in Budapest (Szépmüvészeti Múzeum).[35] The chronology of his other works is largely assigned on the basis of stylistic evolution, and, not surprisingly, Boltraffio's style was most strongly influenced by Leonardo in the last years of the Quattrocento.[36]

The National Gallery's *Virgin and Child* (Plate 3 and Fig. 10) is assigned to this period, and is stylistically associated with the *Girolamo Casio* and *Madonna and Child*, both in Milan (Brera, Plate 11; and Museo Poldi Pezzoli, Plate 12) and a *Virgin and Child* in Budapest (Fig. 11).[37] While the composition of *Girolamo Casio* has its source in the Leonardo *Portrait of a Musician* (Milan, Pinacoteca Ambrosiana), and the three Boltraffio Madonnas mentioned above owe much to Leonardo's '*Litta Madonna*' (St Petersburg, Hermitage), it is clearly evident that in Boltraffio, Leonardo's influence is less literal than in the case of Giampietrino.

In the National Gallery *Virgin and Child*, Boltraffio's more typically creative use of Leonardo's imagery is expressed through an apparently more faithful assimilation of his technique. Most striking is Boltraffio's use of a dark underpainting (Plate 13) of some solidity for much of the composition and this seems to have been a key part of Leonardo's method, and can be seen in a number of unfinished works, such as *The Penitent Saint Jerome* (Rome, Pinacoteca Vaticana) and *The Adoration of the Magi* (Florence, Uffizi). The costume of the Ambrosiana *Musician* is a particularly clear case, where the translucent, brushed quality of the unfinished costume is all the more striking for the contrast with the high degree of finish in the rest of the painting. In the National Gallery *Virgin of the Rocks* a similar dark understructure can be seen through the paint layers in many parts of the picture, and is most clearly evident in the unfinished left hand of the angel. A number of paint cross-sections from the edges of the panel indicate the widespread use of this dark initial painting stage (Plate 14). Boltraffio, like Leonardo, used this dark layer both as a relatively opaque, flat blocking-in of the composition and as a more elaborated undermodelling of form of a type used in the Parma *Head of a Young Girl* (see Plate 9). The presence of Boltraffio's dark underpaint can be seen in the more cracked parts of the picture, particularly underneath the sky and in the land-scape to the left. The layer is apparently thin-ner beneath the areas of flesh and accordingly influences the tonality of these passages less markedly. Analysis of the binding medium shows the main component to be egg tempera with a little oil, with only drying oil (walnut) in the overlying paint layers.[38]

The National Gallery Boltraffio has suffered from some unusual drying faults, which stem from the painting techniques employed. These have resulted both in wide shrinkage fissures, leaving islands of surface paint exposing the underlayers, as well as severe wrinkling in cer-tain areas (Fig. 12).[39] These paint defects are pre-sent over much of the picture surface (with the exception of the dark green cloth-of-honour backdrop which contains siccative copper-green pigments[40]) and, significantly, Boltraffio's por-trait of Girolamo Casio displays similar severe drying defects in the face, hand and hair. Another aspect of the problematic technique of this group of pictures by Boltraffio is the cracked and rather blanched appearance of the blue draperies, visible in the National Gallery and Milan Madonnas. In the former, the Madonna's blue mantle is painted in several layers of azu-rite and ultramarine and the degraded appear-ance is likely to have resulted from both drying problems and deterioration of the pigments. These types of defects are by no means peculiar to Boltraffio, and in fact occur fairly widely throughout Italian panel painting at this time, when the use of the oil medium was still not particularly long established, and its character-istics not well understood.[41] In the case of the National Gallery Boltraffio, the poor drying qualities of the paint might rest on the choice and preparation of walnut oil as the medium. Other factors could be the use of too rich a medium, inadequate drying times between layers, or poor adhesion between incompatible media. Recent analysis of the binding medium of the *Virgin of the Rocks* has shown that Leonardo used solely walnut oil in all the layers, includ-ing the dark undermodelling. Even so, certain areas show severe shrinkage cracking, most notably in the dark cloak of the angel. It is inter-esting to note that the later works of Boltraffio, which reflect different stylistic concerns, are rel-atively free of these disfiguring defects in the paint, and appear more simply painted.[42]

Plate 11 Boltraffio, *Portrait of Girolamo Casio*. Wood, 40 × 52 cm. Milan, Brera.

Plate 12 Boltraffio, *Madonna and Child*. Wood, 45.5 × 35.6 cm. Milan, Museo Poldi Pezzoli.

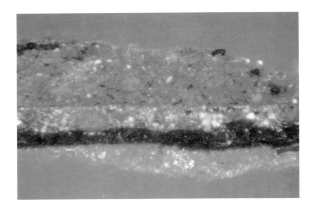

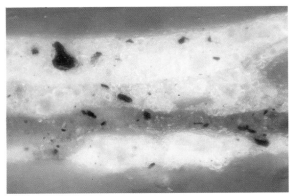

Plate 13 Boltraffio, *The Virgin and Child* (NG 728). Thin cross-section from dark green hanging behind the Virgin showing a glaze, based on verdigris mixed with some charcoal, over a denser green underpaint. Beneath these green layers, and in much of the composition as a whole, there is a dark blackish-brown underlayer, visible here directly over the gesso. Photographed in a combination of reflected and transmitted light. Original magnification 275 ×; actual magnification 240 ×.

Plate 14 Leonardo da Vinci, *The Virgin of the Rocks* (NG 1093). Cross-section from highlight on Saint John's heel, left edge. The flesh paint comprises two layers of light-coloured paint, incorporating a little black pigment, over a translucent dark yellowish-brown underpaint. This underlayer is present beneath large areas of the composition, although not in the sky, and is applied over an off-white *imprimitura*. Original magnification 750 ×; actual magnification 620 ×.

This tentative proposal that Boltraffio's *leonardismo* extended to aspects of his technique is also important in considering the wider phenomenon of Leonardo's influence on other artists. The study of just Giampietrino and Boltraffio hardly constitutes a comprehensive survey of the so-called Leonardesque painters active in Lombardy; even so, comparison between the two reveals something of the variety of reaction to Leonardo and the shifting relationship between style and technique in that response. On one level Giampietrino appears to have seen Leonardo largely as a source of novel compositions, the recycling and repetition of which might suggest a more superficial (or more commercial) interest. There is also a strong influence of Leonardo's striking pictorial effects, expressed through a technique that is much influenced by him, and that can be seen in the *sfumato* and relief of the National Gallery *Christ carrying his Cross* and *Salome* and in the aerial perspective of the landscape of the Kassel *Charity*. Nevertheless, Giampietrino's *leonardismo* is essentially imitative, showing more of an attempted simulation of the painted appearance of Leonardo's works than an understanding of his ideas. Boltraffio, who was never so dependent on Leonardo's compositions, however, seems for a time to have come

Fig. 12 Boltraffio, *The Virgin and Child* (NG 728). Detail of the right edge showing wrinkling and cracking of paint layers resulting from the initial drying process, photographed in raking light.

closer to the underlying principles, technical and otherwise, of Leonardo's painting. It is also tempting to see the problematic condition of Boltraffio's more Leonardesque works as an unfortunate legacy of Leonardo's known technical experimentation. Boltraffio's response to Leonardo would seem the more sophisticated, as he eventually assimilated aspects of his master's painting into a style that was his own; Giampietrino's paintings are on the whole more consistently derivative. Yet Leonardo's painting, resulting as it did from an unprecedented amount of observation and investigation of natural phenomena, remained elusively unreproducible.

Acknowledgements

The authors would like to thank Dr Nicholas Penny, National Gallery; Dr Pietro C. Marani, Pinacoteca di Brera; Dr Andrea di Lorenzo, Museo Poldi Pezzoli; Dr Martina Fleischer, Gemäldegalerie der Akademie der bildenden Künste, Vienna; Dr István Barkóczi, Andras Fáy, and Gábor Pásztov, Szépmüvészeti Múzeum, Budapest; and Dr Cécile Scailliérez, Musée du Louvre, for their kind assistance in arranging to view paintings and providing photographs, and for their helpful discussions of the subject matter. We would also like to thank Dr David Saunders for preparing the superimposed image in Plate 5.

Notes and references

1. See Martin Davies, *The Earlier Italian Schools*, National Gallery Catalogues, London 1961, reprinted 1986, pp. 261–81, and Pietro C. Marani, *Leonardo: Catalogo completo*, Florence 1989.
2. The *Salome* was cleaned and restored in 1993; the *Christ carrying his Cross* in 1994. The *Virgin and Child* by Boltraffio is being restored at the time of writing.
3. See Davies, op. cit., pp. 226–7.
4. Pietro C. Marani, *Leonardo e i leonardeschi a Brera*, Florence 1987, p. 12.
5. G. P. Lomazzo, *Trattato dell'arte della pittura*, Milan 1584, p. 695; on p. 679 he lists a 'Pietro Rizzo Milanesi' among a group of artists 'degni d'essere celebrati, e proposti per essempio ed imitare'.
6. This is the altarpiece of the *Adoration of the Shepherds* in San Marino a Pavia, illustrated in Cristina Geddo, 'Le pale d'altare di Giampietrino: ipotesi per un percorso stilistico', *Arte Lombarda*, 101, 1992, p. 70.
7. See Janice Shell, David Allen Brown, Pinin Brambilla Barcilon, *Giampietrino e una copia cinquecentesca dell'ultima cena di Leonardo*, Milan 1988.
8. The traditional use of this name will be maintained in this article.
9. Geddo, cited in note 6, pp. 67–82.
10. The issue of studio participation had been raised as early as W. Suida, *Leonardo und sein Kreis*, Leipzig 1929, pp. 212–15, 298–302. See also his entry *Pedrini, Giovanni*, in Thieme-Becker, *Allgemeines Lexikon der bildenden Künstler*, 26, Leipzig 1932, pp. 343–4.
11. See Carlo Pedretti, 'Giorgione e il Cristo portacroce di Leonardo', *Almanaco italiano*, 89, 1979, pp. 8–14, and Marani, 'Leonardo e il Cristo portacroce,' *Leonardo e Venezia* (exhibition catalogue), Milan 1992, pp. 344–57.
12. See Marani, *Leonardo e i leonardeschi a Brera*, cited in note 4, pp. 37–43.
13. See Davies, cited in note 1, p. 227.
14. The design was transferred either by blackening the reverse of the cartoon with charcoal or inserting a blackened interleaf between it and the panel, after which the contours of the cartoon were retraced with some sort of blunt stylus.
15. The two pictures show distinct differences in paint handling and level of finish, which provides additional circumstantial evidence for the existence of a large workshop. In general the Budapest picture is much tighter in execution and more precisely and finely modelled in its flesh painting than the rather broadly painted London version (although the simply painted shadow across the extended forearm of the London picture is perhaps a more convincing rendering of the falling shadow), while its drapery painting appears slightly more schematic. Interestingly, another version of clearly lower quality now in the Academy at Vienna is markedly larger in scale and could not have been made from the same cartoon.
16. Pietro C. Marani, 'Per il Giampietrino: nuovi analisi nella pinacoteca di Brera e un grande inedito,' *Raccolta vinciana*, 23, 1989, pp. 36–46.
17. See Pietro Marani's entries in Federico Zeri (ed.), *Pinacoteca di Brera: Scuole lombarda e piemontese 1300–1535*, Milan 1988, pp. 183–4.
18. Leonardo himself developed two variants of the subject in his sketches; a standing figure of the type seen in the da Sesto copy, and a kneeling version (Windsor, Royal Library, n. 12337 r). The Giampietrino *Salome* and *Cleopatra* derive

from the standing Leonardo composition; another Giampietrino in Kassel traditionally identified as a *Leda* but recently redesignated as a *Charity* is the only known painting reflecting Leonardo's kneeling figure. If the subject of the Kassel picture is indeed a *Charity*, as Marani maintains, then it is yet another example of a recycled Leonardo composition for a new subject. See Marani, *Leonardo: Catalogo completo*, cited in note 1, pp. 142–5; Jürgen Lehmann, *Staatliche Kunstsammlungen Kassel: Italienische, französiche und spanische Gemälde des 16. bis 18. Jahrhunderts*, Fridingen 1980, pp. 130–3; A.E. Popham, *The Drawings of Leonardo da Vinci*, London 1994 (revised edition), pp. 56–7; Kenneth Clark, *Leonardo da Vinci*, London 1988 (revised edition), pp. 180–6.

19. The transferred charcoal design, where made by *spolvero* or a tracing method, was presumably brushed away after the elaborated brushed underdrawing.

20. For an overview of the artistic situation in Milan before Leonardo's arrival, see Sydney Freedberg, *Painting in Italy 1500–1600*, Harmondsworth 1975, pp. 381–2.

21. Although poplar is the most common support for Italian panel paintings of the late 15th and early 16th centuries, other wood types, such as walnut, are known for Milanese paintings. Examples in the National Gallery Collection include Boltraffio's *Virgin and Child* (NG 728) discussed in this article, NG 1438 given to a follower of Leonardo, and NG 5752 attributed to de Predis. Jacqueline Marette records a Leonardo panel in the Louvre, *La Belle Feronnière*, as on walnut. See *Connaissance des primitifs par l'étude du bois*, Paris 1961, p. 220.

22. The relatively small amount of carbon-containing black pigment in this layer is enough to somewhat cloud the image of the carbonaceous transferred underdrawing.

23. In this period, modelling of red draperies is usually worked in red lake glazes over underlayers of white, vermilion, vermilion and white or red lake mixed with white. The inclusion of·red earth and black pigment in the Giampietrino *Christ* results in a particularly sombre overall tonality.

24. This practice appears to be quite rare in Italian painting of the period and may be confined to Milanese technique. Final pigmented glazes can be detected in cross-sections and particularly in thin sections by optical means and by analysis, and can be distinguished from old varnish. See Raymond White and Jennifer Pilc, 'Analyses of Paint Media,' *National Gallery Technical Bulletin*, 16, pp. 86–7 and note 11.

25. This attribution, although not universally accepted, is nonetheless widely held. See

Marani, *Leonardo: Catalogo completo*, cited in note 1, p. 110.

26. For a fuller account of the fading of lake pigments see David Saunders and Jo Kirby, 'Light-induced Colour Changes in Red and Yellow Lake Pigments,' *National Gallery Technical Bulletin*, 15, pp. 79–97.

27. Faintly pink translucent flakes of faded lake pigment are just visible under ordinary illumination in several cross-sections, but are revealed more strikingly by their fairly strong orange-pink UV-fluorescence under the microscope.

28. The forehead of Giampietrino's *Madonna and Child* (Milan, Pinacoteca del Castello Sforzesca, inv. 304) is a similar example, well preserved, of this technique of suggesting veiled flesh. See Pietro Marani, *Leonardo e i leonardeschi nei musei della Lombardia*, Milan 1990, p. 137.

29. Something of *Salome*'s lost original richness of surface and colour can be imagined by comparison with *The Magdalen seated in Prayer* (see Plate 4), where the green colour of the book is seemingly unchanged, the red lakes remain well-preserved in the drapery and the flesh paint is distinctly pink. This could be as a result of preservation of the lakes or from the use of inorganic red pigments in the flesh paint. That a noticeably warmer tone for female flesh-painting was commonly employed by Giampietrino can also be supported by the similar rosy appearance of his *Diana* in the Metropolitan Museum in New York.

30. Leonardo wrote extensively on this subject in his notebooks: 'Lights and darks, together with foreshortening, comprise the excellence of the science of painting...Lights and darks, that is to say, illumination and shadow, have an intermediate quality that cannot be called light or dark, but partakes equally of light and dark', or 'Shadows and lights are the most certain means by which the shape of any body comes to be known...', or 'Objects seen in light and shade will be displayed in greater relief than those which are wholly in light or shade,' from Martin Kemp (ed.), *Leonardo on Painting*, London 1989, p. 88. See also Marcia Hall, *Color and Meaning*, Cambridge 1992.

31. See Shell, Brown, and Brambilla Barcilon, cited in note 7.

32. Marani, *Leonardo e i leonardeschi*, cited in note 4, pp. 10–11.

33. Davies, cited in note 1, pp. 88–9.

34. 'Fu discepolo Lionardo Giovanantonio Boltraffio milanese, persona molto practica ed intendente, che l'anno 1500 dipinse in nella chiesa della Misericordia fuor di Bologna in una tavola a olio con grand diligenzia, la Nostra Donna col figliuolo in braccio, San Giovanni Batista, e San Bastiano ignudo, e il padrone che

18

la fe' fare, ritratto di naturale ginocchioni; opera veramente bella; ed in quella scrisse il nome suo e l'esser discepolo de Lionardo.' Giorgio Vasari (ed. Milanesi), *Le vite de più eccellenti pittori, scultori ed architetturi*, Florence 1879, Vol. 4, pp. 51–2.

35. See Giuliano Briganti, *La pittura in Italia: Il cinquecento*, Milan 1988, Vol. 2, p. 727.

36. Leonardo's first Milanese period, as has been stated, lasted until 1499.

37. See Maria Teresa Fiorio's entry in Federico Zeri (ed.), *Pinacoteca di Brera: Scuole lombarda e piemontese 1300–1535*, Milan 1988, pp. 116–18. The 1908 condition report that blamed the poor condition of the *Gerolamo Casio* on it having been placed too near a fire ('la tavoletta appariva abbrustolita per essersi trovata presso il fuoco e imbratata di tinte e vernici') must be disputed in the light of other examples in Boltraffio of problems clearly attributable to painting technique. See also Mauro Natale, *Musei e Gallerie di Milano. Museo Poldi Pezzoli: Dipinti*, Milan 1982, p. 83; and Klara Garas, *A Szépmüvészeti Múzeum kepei*, Budapest 1973, pp. 58, 249.

38. For medium analyses of both the Boltraffio and *The Virgin of the Rocks*, see Raymond White and Jennifer Pilc, 'Analyses of Paint Media', in this *Bulletin*, pp. 96–7.

39. The disrupted surface, changes in colour and loss of pigment resulting from Boltraffio's technique have led to the complete repainting of the Virgin's red tunic, blue mantle, and much of her transparent veil. The use of mastic resin for all these repaints suggests a 19th-century date for this reworking; the repainting of the tunic with kermes lake, generally unavailable in England in the 19th century but apparently still obtainable in continental Europe, suggests a date no later than 1854, when the painting was exported from Italy to the collection of Lord Northwick. See Jo Kirby and Raymond White, 'The Identification of Red Lake Pigment Dyestuffs and a Discussion of their Use' in this *Bulletin*, p. 69.

40. Copper pigments, such as verdigris, appear to have a bi-phasic catalytic action. They appear to enhance the drying rate of drying oils (that is, act as siccatives) and also convert active centres and terminate their production, so functioning as stabilisers or anti-oxidants of the oil paint film.

41. For discussion of another contemporary example of degraded blue paint layer structures, see David Bomford, Janet Brough and Ashok Roy, 'Three Panels from Perugino's Certosa di Pavia Altarpiece', *National Gallery Technical Bulletin*, 4, 1980, pp. 26–8.

42. The 1500 'Casio Altarpiece', painted in Bologna, now in the Louvre, has no dark underlayer in the sky, and appears to be constructed quite conventionally with a thin layer of azurite followed by a modelling layer of azurite and lead white, both applied over a light ground.

Plate 1 Botticelli, *Four Scenes from the Early Life of Saint Zenobius* (NG 3918), *c*.1500. Poplar, 66.5 × 149.8 cm.

Plate 2 Botticelli, *Three Miracles of Saint Zenobius* (NG 3919), *c*.1500. Poplar, 65 × 140.3 cm.

The Materials of a Group of Late Fifteenth-century Florentine Panel Paintings

JILL DUNKERTON AND ASHOK ROY

Introduction

In the past few years six panels all painted in the last quarter of the fifteenth century by Florentine artists have undergone cleaning and restoration in the Conservation Department of the National Gallery, these treatments providing an opportunity to take paint samples for the identification of materials. A seventh panel, *The Virgin and Child with Saint John and Angels* ('*The Manchester Madonna*') by Michelangelo, was examined in connection with the exhibition *Making and Meaning: The Young Michelangelo* (1994/5) and, although it may not have been painted in Florence, it is included in this survey for reasons given below.

As the Table of Results (pp. 24–7) shows, most of the materials are common to all the paintings and differences in their use are generally slight. This should not be surprising, for the artists can be shown to have been linked by more than their city of origin and training.

The two panels by Botticelli, *Four Scenes from the Early Life of Saint Zenobius* and *Three Miracles of Saint Zenobius* (Plates 1 and 2), are from a series of four *spalliere* which have always been accepted as late works. It has been suggested recently that they were painted for the marriage of a member of the Girolami family who claimed descent from the saint's father, and more specifically for the marriage of Zanobi Girolami in 1500[1] – although a narrative in which the first episode shows Zenobius rejecting his prospective bride might seem rather inappropriate for the occasion. In addition, there are some notable differences between the last panel in the sequence, now in Dresden, and the other three.[2] While there can be no doubt that the Dresden picture is from the same series, the figure scale tends to be larger and the range

of colours more limited. Furthermore there is no trace of the shell gold which embellishes costumes and architectural detail in the preceding scenes.

The Virgin and Child with Saint John (Plate 3) by Filippino Lippi is a relatively early work, probably dating from the late 1470s, and therefore painted not long after the period when Filippino had been closely associated with Botticelli. Indeed, it came into the Collection in 1894 as a Botticelli.[3]

The Virgin and Child with an Angel (Plate 4) has been catalogued until recently as by a follower of Botticelli and thought by some to be an early work by him, an attribution based on its similarities with a more widely accepted painting in Naples.[4] Both these pictures are derived from a painting by Filippo Lippi in Florence (Uffizi). On grounds of quality and certain technical features – including a degree of hesitancy, if not incompetence – the National Gallery panel seems unlikely to be associated with Botticelli and it has now reverted to an earlier, more approximate attribution as by an Imitator of Filippo Lippi.[5] It was not necessarily painted in Filippo's lifetime and is quite likely to be close in date to Filippino's little panel.

The attributions of the two arch-topped panels from the Ghirlandaio workshop have also been adjusted. Following cleaning it has become apparent that the *The Virgin and Child* (Plate 5), previously catalogued as 'Studio of Domenico Ghirlandaio', is a beautiful and characteristic work of about 1480 by Domenico himself (as had already been suspected by some scholars).[6] *The Virgin and Child with Saint John* (Plate 6) is now given to Domenico's brother and

21

Plate 3 (*left*) Filippino Lippi, *The Virgin and Child with Saint John* (NG 1412), late 1470s. Poplar, 59.1 × 43.8 cm.

Plate 4 (*below left*) Imitator of Fra Filippo Lippi, *The Virgin and Child with an Angel* (NG 589), *c*.1480. Poplar, 69.9 × 48.3 cm.

business partner, David, a painter whose output has only recently been established with any certainty.[7] The view of Rome in the background suggests that it is likely to have been painted after 1482 when the Ghirlandaio brothers returned from working alongside Botticelli in the Sistine Chapel. Botticelli and Domenico were near contemporaries and are also thought to have been associated with the large and busy workshop of Verrocchio at about the same time.

In its turn Domenico's workshop became the training ground for a significant proportion of the next generation of artists, including, most famously, the young Michelangelo. There is a possibility that the '*Manchester Madonna*' (Plate 7) was begun in Rome in 1497, but an earlier date cannot be excluded.[8] In technique the panel emerges as entirely within the tradition of the Ghirlandaio workshop.

This technical tradition, which is also that of Botticelli and Filippino Lippi (at least in the earlier part of his career), is relatively conservative. Although, as the Table of Results shows, some oil was used for specific colours, the panels were executed with what was still in its essentials an egg-tempera technique, retaining the characteristic light and brilliant tonality, and often making extensive use of gilded decoration. They seem to have rejected – perhaps quite consciously – the more innovative and experimental development of the properties of the oil medium as exploited by, for example, the Pollaiuoli brothers, Leonardo da Vinci and even the more conservative artist Perugino. In panels such as those for the Certosa di Pavia,[9] Perugino made use of glazes in a manner approaching that of Netherlandish painters to achieve both depth of tone and optical complexity.

Plate 5 Domenico Ghirlandaio, *The Virgin and Child* (NG 3937), *c.*1480. Poplar, 92.3 × 58 cm (including modern addition at the top of the arch).

Plate 6 David Ghirlandaio, *The Virgin and Child with Saint John* (NG 2502), 1480s. Poplar, 78.8 × 46.5 cm.

Plate 7 (*right*) Michelangelo, *The Virgin and Child with Saint John and Angels* ('*The Manchester Madonna*') (NG 809), perhaps 1497. Poplar, 104.5 × 77 cm.

Table of Results

ARTIST/PAINTING	Botticelli, *Four Scenes from the Early Life of Saint Zenobius* (NG 3918)	Botticelli, *Three Miracles of Saint Zenobius* (NG 3919)	Filippino Lippi, *The Virgin and Child with Saint John* (NG 1412)
SUPPORT	Poplar, presumed	Poplar, presumed	Poplar, identified[1]
GROUND[3]	Gesso	Gesso	Gesso
UNDERDRAWING	Particles of **vegetable black**[4] visible in some cross-sections. Fine brush drawing to delineate contours and folds visible in infra-red. Architectural elements incised.	Particles of **vegetable black** visible in some cross-sections. Fine brush drawing to delineate contours and folds visible in infra-red. Architectural elements incised.	Some broad lines of brush drawing visible in infra-red. Parapet incised.
BLUE	Sleeve of Zenobius rejecting his bride: **azurite** and **lead white**, traces of **natural ultramarine** in shadow. Sky: **azurite** and **lead white** in **egg**.[6]	Blue areas not sampled for pigments. **Azurite** found in purple mixture. Sky, medium: **egg**.[6] Blue tunic of man in central group, medium: **egg**.[6]	Virgin's mantle: mid-tone, **natural ultramarine** and **lead white**, probably in **egg**,[6] over **lead white** local *imprimitura*; shadow, as above but with additional **natural ultramarine** glaze in **linseed oil**.[6] Sky: **azurite** and **lead white** in **egg**.[6]
GREEN	Dark green carpet: **artificial malachite**[7] in **egg**, with some **walnut oil**.[6] Green and yellow *cangiante* robe of the rejected bride: mid-tone, **artificial malachite** and **lead-tin yellow**.[8]	Dark green sleeve of beggar, far right: **artificial malachite** and **lead-tin yellow**.	Lining of Virgin's mantle: **artificial malachite** in **egg**[6] over **lead white** local *imprimitura*. Sample for medium analysis also included a **copper green** glaze in **linseed oil**.[6] Foliage between Saint John and the Virgin: **artificial malachite** over black underpaint.[9] Tree on top of grass, right edge: **azurite** over **artificial malachite** and **lead-tin yellow**.
RED, PINK AND RED-BROWN	Opaque red draperies: **vermilion**. Pink-brown floor, right-hand episode: **vermilion** and **lead white**. Red-brown urn at baptism of Zenobius: **vermilion**, **vegetable black** and **lead white**, modelled with **vermilion** and **vegetable black**.	Opaque reds not sampled. Pink of cope of Zenobius, left-hand episode: **red lake** in **egg** with a little oil.[6]	Pink of Saint John's drapery: **red lake**, dyestuff identified as **lac**,[12] in **walnut oil**.[6]

Imitator of Fra Filippo Lippi, *The Virgin and Child with an Angel* (NG 589)	Domenico Ghirlandaio, *The Virgin and Child* (NG 3937)	David Ghirlandaio, *The Virgin and Child with Saint John* (NG 2502)	Michelangelo, *The Virgin and Child with Saint John and Angels* ('The Manchester Madonna') (NG 809)
Poplar, presumed	Poplar, presumed	Poplar, presumed	Poplar, identified[2]
Gesso	Gesso	Gesso	Gesso
Particles of **vegetable black** visible in some cross-sections. Broad lines of brush drawing visible in infra-red. Architectural elements incised.	Particles of **vegetable black** visible in some cross-sections. Brush drawing to delineate contours and folds visible in infra-red.[5] Arch incised.	Particles of **vegetable black** visible in some cross-sections. Fine brush drawing and some broader lines of wash to indicate contours and folds visible in infra-red.[5] Lines of **red lake** visible in damaged areas of Virgin's mantle. Arch incised.	Brush drawing with **vegetable black** in an aqueous medium (**egg**?) to indicate contours and folds visible in unpainted areas and in infra-red.[5]
Virgin's mantle: two layers of **natural ultramarine** and **lead white** in **egg**[6] over **lead white** local *imprimitura*.	Virgin's mantle: highlight, **azurite** and **lead white**; shadow, **azurite** in **walnut oil**.[6] Sky: **natural ultramarine** and **lead white**.	Virgin's mantle: **natural ultramarine** and **lead white** in **egg**.[6] Sky: **natural ultramarine** and **lead white**.	Sky: **azurite** and **lead white** in **egg**.[6]
Lining of Virgin's mantle: **artificial malachite** and **lead-tin yellow**, traces of discoloured 'copper resinate' type glaze, over **lead white** local *imprimitura*. Grass to left of angel's waist: **artificial malachite** and **lead-tin yellow** over layer of **lead white** to cover *pentimento*.[10] Grass in distant landscape: **artificial malachite**.	Lining of Virgin's mantle: mid-tone, **artificial malachite**; shadow, **artificial malachite** with discoloured 'copper resinate' type glaze. Dark green lattice pattern on textile: medium, **walnut oil**.[6] Grass in landscape on right: **artificial malachite** and **lead-tin yellow**. Tree on right: **artificial malachite**, **azurite** and **natural malachite** with a discoloured 'copper resinate' type glaze.	Lining of Virgin's mantle: **natural malachite** (rosasite).[11] Brown-green of grass on left: **artificial malachite**, **lead-tin yellow** and **yellow earth** over **natural malachite** (rosasite) and **artificial malachite**. Tree on left: **artificial malachite** (discoloured) and a little **natural ultramarine** with a discoloured 'copper resinate' type glaze in **linseed oil**.[6]	Lining of Virgin's mantle: **natural malachite**. Grass in foreground: **natural malachite**, sometimes with some **lead-tin yellow**, in **egg** with a little **oil**.[6] Pale green of *cangiante* sash of angel on far right: **natural malachite** and **lead white**.
Book, lower right: **vermilion**. Virgin's dress: **red lake** in **egg**[6] over **lead white** local *imprimitura*.	Virgin's dress: **red lake**, identified as **lac** with a little **kermes**[12] mixed with **lead white** in the highlights. Shadowed area of red stripe on textile: **vermilion** glazed with **red lake** in **egg** (probably in the underlayer) and **walnut oil** (in the glaze).[6]	Virgin's dress: **red lake**, identified as **kermes** with a little **lac**.[12] Saint John's red drapery: **red lake** over **red lake** and **lead white**. Red area of carpet: **vermilion** in **egg** glazed with **red lake**, dyestuff identified as **lac**,[12] in **linseed oil**.[6]	Virgin's dress and tunic of angel on far right: **red lake** dyestuff identified as **lac** possibly with a little **kermes**,[12] in **egg** and **walnut oil**.[6] Red of *cangiante* sash of angel on far right: **vermilion**. Red shadows of *cangiante* tunic of angel second from right: **vermilion**.

ARTIST/PAINTING	Botticelli (NG 3918)	Botticelli (NG 3919)	Filippino Lippi (NG 1412)
YELLOW AND YELLOW-BROWN	Green and yellow *cangiante* robe of the rejected bride: highlight, **lead-tin yellow**[8] and **yellow earth**.	Cloak of blind beggar on right: highlight, **lead-tin yellow** over **lead-tin yellow** and **yellow earth**; shadow, **lead-tin yellow**, **yellow earth**, **lead white** and a little **vermilion**. Green mixtures contain **lead-tin yellow**.	Green mixtures contain **lead-tin yellow**.
BLACK, GREY, PURPLE AND PURPLE-GREY	Lilac drapery of woman, far left: **natural ultramarine**, **red lake** and **lead white**. Purple-grey pilaster: **vegetable black**, **vermilion** and **lead white**.	Purple robe of figure running down steps: **azurite**, **red lake** and **lead white** with (in the shadows) a glaze of **red lake**, **vermilion** and **vegetable black**. Shoe of acolyte to left of Zenobius in central episode: **vegetable black** over **lead white**, black and a little **red earth**. Shoe of youth having devil driven out, on left: **vegetable black**, **lead white** and a little **red earth**.	Christ Child's mauve drapery: three layers of **azurite**, **red lake** and **lead white** (the **red lake** has faded in the upper layer).
FLESH	Translucent brown shadow of forearm of Saint Sophia: **yellow earth**,[15] **vegetable black** and **lead white**. Underpaint: **lead white**.	Not sampled.	Saint John's upper arm, junction between highlight and shadow: **lead white** with a little **vermilion** over a translucent brown consisting of **yellow earth**,[15] **vegetable black** and **lead white**. Underpaint: **green earth** and **lead white**.
GILDING	**Shell gold.** Sample from hem of lilac drapery of woman, far left.	**Shell gold** – not sampled.	**Mordant gilding** – not sampled.

Notes to the Table of Results

1. The wood of the panel was misidentified in 1917 as American basswood or butternut and the picture designated a forgery. The wood was correctly identified in 1935. See p. 30, note 1 (Davies p. 288).
2. Identified by Joyce Plesters.
3. The gesso grounds have been examined by X-ray diffraction analysis; in general a mixture of gypsum and anhydrite is found. Because of the inhomogeneity of the grounds, the proportions vary.
4. Microscopically these black pigments are carbonised plant materials, but do not exhibit the particle character of wood charcoal.
5. For infra-red images, see p. 30, note 6.
6. For fuller media results for NG 3918, 3919, 3937, 2502 and 809, see R. White and J. Pilc, 'Analyses of Paint Media', *National Gallery Technical Bulletin*, 16, 1995, pp. 86-7; for NG 1412, see pp. 96–7 of this *Bulletin*; and for NG 589 see J. Mills and R. White, 'Analyses of Paint Media', *National Gallery Technical Bulletin*, 12, 1988, pp. 78–9.
7. Artificial malachite ($CuCO_3.Cu(OH)_2$) is distinguished from its natural counterpart by a distinctly globular particle form, variable particle size and the occurrence of fused spherulites. For fuller details see p. 31, notes 14–16.
8. Lead-tin yellow identified microscopically and by EDX (Pb, Sn). In two cases (yellow samples from NG 3937 and 2502), the 'type I' form of lead-tin yellow was confirmed by XRD. EDX results for the remainder suggest 'type I' in all cases.
9. This is a traditional method for constructing dark foliage and landscape greens in tempera paintings.

Imitator of Fra Filippo Lippi (NG 589)	Domenico Ghirlandaio (NG 3937)	David Ghirlandaio (NG 2502)	Michelangelo (NG 809)
Green mixtures contain **lead-tin yellow**.	Cushion: highlight, **lead-tin yellow**; shadow, **yellow** and **red earths** and a little **vermilion in egg**.[6] Green mixtures contain **lead-tin yellow**.	Yellow-brown of Saint John's cross: **lead-tin yellow, yellow earth** and a little **vegetable black**. Green mixtures contain **lead-tin yellow**.	*Cangiante* tunic of angel second from right: highlight, **lead-tin yellow**; midtone and underlayer, **yellow earth**. Green mixtures contain **lead-tin yellow**.
Angel's purple tunic: **azurite, red lake** and **lead white** in several layers over **lead white** local *imprimitura*. Pale purple-grey of table, right foreground: **azurite, red lake** and **lead white**. Pink-grey of distant mountains: **vegetable black, vermilion** and/or **red earth** and **lead white**. Warm grey of architecture: **lead white**, finely ground **vegetable black** and a little **yellow earth** in **egg**.[6]	Purple-grey of stone of arch: mid-tone, **lampblack**(?),[13] **red lake** and **lead white**; shadow, as mid-tone but with glaze of **charcoal black**,[14] **red lake** and **azurite**.	Purple-grey of stone of arch: highlight, **natural ultramarine, red lake** and **lead white** over **natural ultramarine, red lake** and **vegetable black**; shadow, **natural ultramarine, red lake** and **vegetable black**.	Black undermodelling of Virgin's mantle: **vegetable black** in **egg**.[6] Purple-grey of angel's wing and area between heads of angels on right: **vegetable black, red lake** and **lead white**.
Highlights of Christ Child's foot and thigh: **lead white** with a little **vermilion**. Shadow of foot: **vermilion, lead white** and **vegetable black**. Underpaint: **yellow earth, vegetable black** and **lead white** (*verdaccio*) over **lead white** local *imprimitura*.	Virgin's forehead, junction between highlight and shadow: **lead white** with a little **vermilion** over a translucent brown.[16] Highlight on Virgin's collarbone: **lead white** with a little **vermilion**. Christ Child's right hand, medium: **egg**.[6] Underpaint: **green earth** and **lead white**.	Highlight on top of Christ's foot: **lead white**. Virgin's cheek: **lead white** over **lead white** with a little **vermilion**. Saint John's left arm, medium: **egg**.[6] Underpaint: **green earth** and **lead white**.	Christ's forearm, mid-tone: **lead white** with a little **vermilion** and **red earth**, followed by a thin layer of translucent brown. Underpaint: **green earth** and **lead white**.
Mordant gilding. Mordant from neckline of Virgin's dress: **vegetable black, vermilion** and **red earth**.	**Mordant gilding.** Mordant from neckline of Virgin's dress: **brown earth** and **lead white** with a high proportion of medium.	**Mordant gilding.** Mordant from Saint John's drapery: **brown earth** and **lead white** with a high proportion of medium.	Not present.

10. Cross-sections from NG 589 (for example Plate 9) often show many paint layers which result both from *pentimenti* and adjustments to outlines; intermediate layers of lead white are used in areas where the design has been modified.
11. Rosasite is a rare mineral closely related to malachite, in which a proportion of the copper atoms are replaced by zinc $((Cu,Zn)CO_3.Cu(OH)_2)$. For fuller details see text and p. 31, note 17.
12. For fuller results of HPLC analysis of red lakes, see pp. 68-70 of this *Bulletin*. In two cases (NG 3937 and 2502) the lake substrates were examined by EDX; strong peaks for aluminium and calcium were recorded.
13. Lampblack suspected from the very fine, even, rounded grains.

14. Typical angular and splintered wood charcoal fragments.
15. The yellow components of these brown flesh tones appear to be translucent forms of earth pigment; a proportion of yellow lake pigment, however, cannot be excluded.
16. The underlayer here is so thin ($c. 2\mu$) that the individual components cannot be discerned even at high magnification under the microscope; however, the appearance both on the painting and in cross-section suggests the same constitution noted for NG 3918 and 1412.

Commentary on results

The most immediately striking feature of the Table of Results is the consistent occurrence of the same materials throughout the paintings surveyed and also how limited these materials are in range, even allowing for the relatively restricted palette available in the fifteenth century.[10] Apart from the inevitable uses of lead white and carbon blacks, the same few pigments appear repeatedly, both on their own and as components of very similar mixtures. The two blue pigments, ultramarine and azurite, seem to be used interchangeably on both skies and draperies so that in Botticelli's panels we find azurite skies and draperies (ultramarine is reserved for the deepest shadows and for some of the purple mixtures),[11] and in the Madonnas of David Ghirlandaio and the Imitator of Filippo Lippi, ultramarine was used for all blue areas. Filippino combines an azurite sky with an ultramarine drapery; the converse is found on Domenico's panel. Michelangelo's intentions for the unfinished mantle of the Virgin in the 'Manchester Madonna' are not known of course, but the pattern set by the paintings discussed here suggests that the black underpainting could have been completed either with ultramarine or azurite.

Only two types of red pigment appear: the opaque red, vermilion, and red lakes. In all cases where analysis has been possible, the dyestuffs have been found to derive principally from lac, with the exception of David Ghirlandaio's panel where the Virgin's dress was found to contain a kermes lake. The glaze on the carpet, however, was lac. As kermes was considerably more expensive than lac, in this instance there may have been a deliberate distinction between the two dyestuffs. On the other hand, in the paintings by Domenico Ghirlandaio and Michelangelo analysis suggests that there may be small amounts of kermes with the lac lake (see pp. 68–70 of this *Bulletin*). Since the dyestuffs are similar in appearance and colour, both as dry powders and when used as a paint, and the addition of kermes would not significantly modify the colour of the lac, here it seems more likely that the combination was accidental.

The lead-tin yellow (artificial lead-tin oxide) which appears in all these paintings was a standard material, but by this time only the 'type I' was used,[12] in contrast to the regular appearance of the 'type II' pigment (Cennino's *giallorino*), based on glass manufacture, found widely in Florentine altarpieces of the fourteenth century.[13]

With the exception of the specific role of green earth, the only green pigment to occur is malachite. In fifteenth-century Italian painting, malachite for greens, in one form or another, became a standard part of the palette and is widely used for draperies, landscape and foliage, replacing the mixtures for green that had been the principal method in the trecento. By the sixteenth century, with the dominance of oil medium, verdigris was preferred. The lack of alternatives to make satisfactory greens in tempera – verdigris works rather poorly in egg and the type of *terra verde* available at this period was too weak in colour for most purposes other than for underpainting flesh – presumably encouraged the use of malachite, which functions reliably well in egg. Particularly evident is an artificial form of the pigment (Plates 8 and 9), characterised by a distinctive spherulitic particle morphology[14] that arises from preparation by precipitation from soluble copper salts in an aqueous solution using calcium carbonate (chalk).[15] Artificial malachite of this type is not confined to Florentine paintings. It has been detected in a number of panel paintings of the fifteenth century, including those by Sienese, Venetian and Ferrarese painters, for example Sassetta, Bellini, Cosimo Tura and Cossa, but it is wholly typical of the workshops that owe their technical traditions to Florence, going back at least as far as Uccello.[16] Ground mineral malachite, as a dry pigment, was probably indistinguishable from the artificial equivalent, unless the natural material was coarsely ground and of a notably strong colour, as used for the lining of the Virgin's cloak (Plate 10) in the 'Manchester Madonna'.

The identification in the lining of the Virgin's mantle (Plate 11) of David Ghirlandaio's *Virgin and Child with Saint John* of the rare copper- and zinc-containing analogue of malachite, known as rosasite,[17] is an unusual occurrence, but it is unlikely that this rare material was recognised as anything other than malachite, perhaps of a particularly favourable tone, and it is significant that artificial malachite occurs also in the same

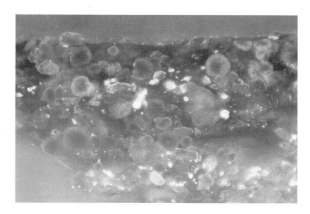

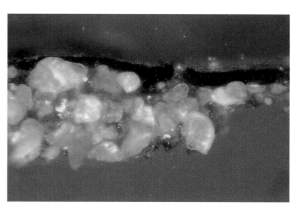

Plate 8 Filippino Lippi, *The Virgin and Child with Saint John* (NG 1412). Cross-section from the mid-green lining of the Virgin's mantle showing the characteristic spherulitic particle form of artificial malachite. Original magnification 600 ×; actual magnification 500 ×.

Plate 10 Michelangelo, *The Virgin and Child with Saint John and Angels* ('*The Manchester Madonna*') (NG 809). Cross-section from a point where the hem of the robe of the angel on the far right overlaps the green of the grass, showing a thin layer of red lake over coarsely ground particles of natural (mineral) malachite. Original magnification 275 ×; actual magnification 240 ×.

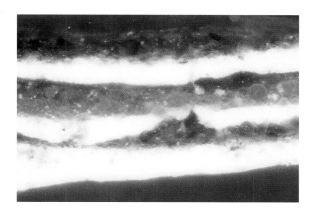

Plate 9 Imitator of Fra Filippo Lippi, *The Virgin and Child with Saint John* (NG 589). Cross-section from blue-green of Virgin's cloak, between Saint John's legs showing an intermediate paint layer (pentimento) composed of artificial (spherulitic) malachite. The surface paint is natural ultramarine and the complex layer structure arises from a series of original modifications to the design made in the course of execution. Intermediate stages were obliterated with layers of lead white. Original magnification 390 ×; actual magnification 310 ×.

Plate 11 David Ghirlandaio, *The Virgin and Child with Saint John* (NG 2502). Cross-section from lining of the Virgin's dark green mantle painted in natural (mineral) malachite containing substituted zinc (rosasite). Original magnification 240 ×; actual magnification 220 ×.

picture in the background landscape. It is possible that this group of green pigments was regarded by the suppliers and users as interchangeable materials.

The suppliers of these varieties of malachite, and of the other pigments, were most probably the Gesuati friars of San Giusto alle Mure. Botticelli, Ghirlandaio and Michelangelo are among the many Florentine artists documented as having obtained pigments from them, while

there is indirect evidence to suggest that Filippino was also a customer (as was his father).[18]

A similar consistent pattern appears in the choice of media. In all the paintings the lighter colours, including the skies, the flesh painting and areas of yellow and white,[19] are in pure egg tempera. With the exception of the painter of the *Virgin and Child with an Angel* (Plate 4) who seems to have used egg throughout (at least in the colours sampled), all the artists employed some drying oil for darker and more transparent shades of red, green and blue. It is not always easy to determine by analysis whether the oil and egg have been used in distinct layers or whether the oil has been incorporated into the egg to make an enriched tempera or *tempera grassa*. However, examples of the former would seem to include the final ultramarine glaze on the blue mantle in Filippino's Virgin and the azurite blue mantle of the Virgin in the panel by Domenico Ghirlandaio, where the pigment has been applied entirely in walnut oil. Several of the paintings include 'copper resinate'-type glazes containing oil, but in the case of the dark greens in the two Botticelli panels and in the '*Manchester Madonna*' the oil seems to have been added to the egg in small quantities. Analysis suggests that *tempera grassa* is also the medium for the red lakes in these three paintings. The rich red glazes on the textiles draped over the parapets in the two panels by the Ghirlandaio brothers are both based on oil, and also the pink of Saint John's drapery in Filippino's panel. Filippino was later to make increasing use of the oil medium in his paintings.[20]

The composition of the flesh tones in the paintings we have surveyed is directly comparable since all the samples are from the flesh of women and young children (the inclusion of older male figures might have increased the variety). In every case the highlights consist of lead white lightly pigmented with vermilion.[21] The appearance of the thin and delicate touches of translucent brown used to model the midtones and shadows on most of the panels is very similar, both in surface appearance and in cross-sections. Where the layer is sufficiently substantial for the components to be recognised under the microscope, it can be seen to contain yellow earth, vegetable black and lead white, a traditional mixture for flesh painting called *verdaccio* by Cennino. The only painting with a slightly different composition to the darker flesh tones is that now attributed to an Imitator of Filippo Lippi in which a mixture of vermilion, vegetable black and lead white is used. In this work the cooler effects were obtained by the use of a *verdaccio* mixture as an underpainting for the flesh areas. The flesh tones in the panels by Botticelli are applied over a layer

of pure lead white. All the others are underpainted with green earth and lead white. The survival of this highly traditional technique through to the last years of the fifteenth century is particularly associated with the Ghirlandaio workshop.[22] Filippino, for example, seems to have abandoned it by about 1480, soon after the probable date of execution of his National Gallery panel.

The technique of mordant gilding is equally traditional. Only in the panels by Botticelli is there any shell (powdered) gold, but he often used mordant gilding as well.[23] The mordants employed by the two Ghirlandaio brothers, not unexpectedly, are identical in constitution, and similar coloured mordants can be seen on many products of their workshop. The mordant in the panel given to an Imitator of Filippo Lippi is more unusual and again suggests a slight separation between this painting and the rest of the group in this survey. However, it is only in such small details that the materials found can begin to indicate differences between the various workshops, let alone between individual painters.

Acknowledgements

The authors would like to thank Marika Spring and Jilleen Nadolny for their help with technical examination and analysis; Raymond White for medium analysis and Jo Kirby for identification of the red lake pigment dyestuffs; and Nicholas Penny for advice on the text.

Notes and references

1. E. Callman, 'Botticelli's "Life of Saint Zenobius"', *The Art Bulletin*, LXVI, 1984, pp. 492–5. For other suggestions as to their original location see M. Davies, *The Earlier Italian Schools*, National Gallery Catalogues, London 1961, reprinted 1986, p. 109.
2. For large colour reproductions of the panels in Dresden and New York (the latter is the least well-preserved of the four), see R. Lightbown, *Sandro Botticelli: Life and Work*, London 1989, plates 111 and 112.
3. Davies, cited in note 1, p. 288.
4. Davies, cited in note 1, pp. 113–14.
5. It entered the Collection in 1857 as a work by Filippo Lippi.
6. For a fuller discussion of this painting with a note on its cleaning, see M. Hirst and J. Dunkerton, *Making and Meaning: The Young Michelangelo*, London 1994, pp. 86ff and p. 128, note 9.

7. See Hirst and Dunkerton, cited in note 6, pp. 86ff and p. 128, notes 8 and 10.
8. Hirst and Dunkerton, cited in note 6, pp. 37ff and pp. 83ff.
9. For the technique of these panels see D. Bomford, J. Brough and A. Roy, 'Three Panels from Perugino's Certosa di Pavia Altarpiece', *National Gallery Technical Bulletin*, 4, 1980, pp. 3–31. An account of the treatment (with some observations on the technique) of another panel in the Collection given to Perugino has also been published (D. Bomford, 'Perugino's "Virgin and Child with Saint John"', *National Gallery Technical Bulletin*, 1, 1977, pp. 29–34). However, the attribution of this panel to Perugino is now doubted, partly because of the removal during cleaning of a spurious inscription from the Virgin's mantle, but principally because of contradictions between the style which would appear to be late, perhaps around or after 1500, and the technique which is conservative and quite unlike that of Perugino's works of the 1490s. Indeed the technique is directly comparable with that of the panels studied in this survey and includes the use of natural malachite.
10. For the range of pigments available in the fourteenth and fifteenth centuries, see D. Bomford, J. Dunkerton, D. Gordon and A. Roy, *Art in the Making: Italian Painting Before 1400*, London 1989, pp. 30–43, and J. Dunkerton, S. Foister, D. Gordon and N. Penny, *Giotto to Dürer: Early Renaissance Painting in the National Gallery*, London 1991, pp. 182–7.
11. Botticelli frequently used ultramarine on other works. For a comparative survey of the technique of several paintings, mainly in Florence, see M. Ciatti (ed.), *'L'Incoronazione della Vergine' del Botticelli: restauro e ricerche*, Florence 1990, pp. 81–109. A study of the technique of *The Adoration of the Kings* (NG 592), usually taken to be an early work by Botticelli, was published in 1955 (see H. Ruhemann, 'Technical analysis of an early painting by Botticelli', *Studies in Conservation*, II, 1955, pp. 17–40). A few cross-sections were prepared but the study is based principally on an examination made using a stereo binocular microscope, supported by photographic techniques. The observations (which are not entirely consistent with the evidence of the samples as presented) need to be confirmed by more up-to-date methods of examination and analysis.
12. Lead-tin yellow 'type I' appears to have been a product of Northern Europe, specifically Germany, as one early name – *giallo tedesco* – implies, although the technology of manufacture was almost certainly adopted in Italy. See H. Kühn, 'Lead-Tin Yellow' in *Artists' Pigments. A Handbook of Their History and Characteristics*, Vol.2, rev. and ed. by A. Roy, Washington D.C. 1993, pp. 86–9 and 99–110; also, E. Martin and A.R. Duval, 'Les deux variétés de jaune de plomb et d'étain: étude chronologique', *Studies in Conservation*, 35, 1990, pp. 117–36.
13. See D. Bomford et al, cited in note 10, pp. 37–9.
14. See R.J. Gettens and E.W. FitzHugh, 'Malachite and Green Verditer' in A. Roy, 1994, cited in note 12, pp. 194–5, particularly Figs. 12, 13, 14 and 15C. EDX spot analysis on individual pigment particles yield strong peaks for copper and little else.
15. P. Mactaggart and A. Mactaggart, 'Refiners' verditer', *Studies in Conservation*, 25, 1980, pp. 38–40.
16. Artificial malachite is present in foliage and landscape of Uccello's *Battle of San Romano* (NG 583) probably from the 1450s. It may also occur on an earlier panel, in foreground paint of Masaccio's *Saints Jerome and John the Baptist* (NG 5962) of the late 1420s.
17. Another occurrence is reported in E. Martin and M. Eveno, 'Contribution to the study of old green copper pigments in easel paintings', *3rd International Conference on Non-Destructive Testing, Microanalytical Methods and Environment Evaluation for Study and Conservation of Works of Art*, Viterbo 1992, pp. 781–91.
18. P. Bensi, 'Gli arnesi dell'arte. I Gesuati di San Giusto alle Mura e la pittura del rinascimento a Firenze', *Studi di Storia delle arti*, III, 1980, pp. 33–47.
19. Samples of white or cream-coloured paint not included in the Table were taken from NG 3918, 3919 and 589. All were egg. For references see Notes to Table (note 6).
20. Results have been published showing walnut and linseed oils, with some egg in lighter colours and in underpaints, in two panels in the Collection which were then catalogued as by Filippino (NG 4094 and 4095; see J. Mills and R. White, 'Organic Analysis in the Arts: Some Further Paint Medium Analyses', *National Gallery Technical Bulletin*, 2, 1978, pp. 74–5). Although they are now assigned to a Follower of Filippino, possibly the Master of Tavernelle who may be a painter called Niccolò Cartoni (see E. Fahy, *Some Followers of Domenico Ghirlandaio*, New York and London 1976, p. 201), this use of media probably reflects Filippino's later workshop practice.
21. The layers of pure lead white which occur in the samples of flesh paint from the panel by David Ghirlandaio are a consequence of his application of the tempera with very precise and distinctly separated brushstrokes. The pinker tones are of the same composition as on the other paintings.
22. See Hirst and Dunkerton, cited in note 6, pp. 96–7.
23. See Ciatti, cited in note 11, p. 103 for a useful table of Botticelli's gilding methods.

Plate 1 Paolo Veronese, *Allegory of Love, II* ('Scorn') (NG 1324), 1570s. Canvas. Detail of Plate 3.

Veronese's Paintings in the National Gallery Technique and Materials: Part II

NICHOLAS PENNY, ASHOK ROY AND MARIKA SPRING

Introduction

In the first part of this article published in Volume 16 of the *Technical Bulletin*, Veronese's early painting of *Christ with a Kneeling Woman*, his mature altarpiece for San Benedetto Po near Mantua of *The Consecration of Saint Nicholas*, and one of the greatest of all his heroic narrative paintings, *The Family of Darius before Alexander*, were examined. Although the last of these three works is not dated, it seems to us likely to be a work of the 1560s and in this second part of the article we will examine the series of four *Allegories of Love* (NG 1318, 1324–6) and the painting of *Saint Helena* (NG 1041) which belong, we believe, to the 1570s, as well as *The Adoration of the Kings* (NG 268) which is dated 1573.

The Allegories of Love

Veronese, after initial successes in his native Verona and elsewhere in the mainland provinces of Venice in the 1540s, moved to Venice in the 1550s to paint canvases for ceilings in the Ducal Palace and in the sacristy and nave of the church of San Sebastiano. He was also one of the group of artists chosen to paint canvases for the roundels in the ceiling of the Marciana Library and his were esteemed the finest of these and awarded a prize by Titian. Although he painted important altarpieces in Venice, it was perhaps his skill as a ceiling painter which first made a great impression on his contemporaries. If we exclude works in public buildings, nothing of this kind survives in good condition in a palace or villa with the exception of the ceilings frescoed by him in the Villa Barbaro at Maser. But we may feel sure that the four approximately square canvases in the National Gallery (Plates 2–5) originally served, or were intended to serve, as ceiling decoration.

These four paintings were first recorded in a posthumous inventory of the collection of the Holy Roman Emperor, Rudolph II.[1] They were not included in an earlier inventory, perhaps because they were not regarded as portable items but were incorporated into a ceiling in Prague Castle (or set aside with the intention of being incorporated). In Venice ceiling compartments were generally more complex shapes and no ceiling of four square compartments, or even four principal compartments, is recorded,[2] so Veronese may have been working to the plans of Rudolph's architect, or may have considered that there was some virtue in simplicity when working for a site he could never have seen. That the paintings were intended for a ceiling, rather than for display high on a wall, is confirmed by two features. Firstly, the architectural elements within them are shown tilted at an angle, which always looks awkward in paintings hung more or less vertically. Secondly, the lower part of the compositions seem to have been cut, and in several cases the feet of some of the figures are invisible. This is usual in a ceiling painting, but very disconcerting in paintings hung on a wall.

The composition of each picture forms a strong diagonal, which would help on a ceiling to relate the paintings to each other (as in the arrangement in Fig. 1) but could serve no such purpose on a wall. This device is obvious enough in all four pictures, but is most ingenious and most subtly dramatic in the painting of the naked man being beaten by a cupid ('Scorn', Plates 1 and 3) where there is a double diagonal – the line of the bank and the outstretched arm of the statue is paralleled by the thigh and forearm of the principal woman, the wings of the cupid and the broken statue of a faun – against which the women's heads, the head and body of the cupid, the raised arm of the man and the tree trunk are contrasted. Veronese's love of diagonals is evident in paintings by him of all types, but what is distinctive here is the relative unimportance of verticals and horizontals.

A sheet of preliminary figure studies in pen and ink with wash (Fig. 2) includes designs for figures and figure groups in all four paintings, which shows that the compositions were developed simultaneously.[3] It also shows that the compositions were essentially figure groups – trees and architecture, which might be fundamental scaffolding for a composition, are here accessories. The drawing also suggests one other practice of great interest. The wedded couple in 'Happy Union' (Plate 5) were originally conceived as advancing from the left – the more usual direction for action in a picture – but were then reversed in the painting, presumably to balance the diagonal movement in the other pictures.

Rudolph, who is known to have admired Veronese's paintings intensely,[4] is likely to have commissioned these four allegories soon after he became emperor in 1576 and it is tempting to suppose that they were made to decorate a marriage bedchamber, for the subjects, although they have never been completely and convincingly explained, are certainly connected with the trials and rewards of love.[5] They are as obscure and elaborate as the subjects Rudolph usually favoured, but rather more edifying, with lust explicitly subdued in one scene, restraint apparently exercised in another, monogamy perhaps selected in a third and fidelity certainly celebrated in a fourth. If the paintings did play a part in such a setting then the centre of the ceiling would certainly have been likely to display the couple's united arms. And it has been ingeniously observed that the men in each picture may have been intended to gaze at such an heraldic centrepiece.[6] Certainly some explanation has to be found for them staring out of the paintings. The only problem – a very considerable one – is that the Emperor never married.

The fact that these paintings were intended for a ceiling explains some passages of very broad and summary handling, especially in the foliage, but also in the lights on the drapery. Clearly these passages might have been left to studio assistants. However, work such as this, although rapidly executed, needed to be carefully judged, and would surely have been delegated with reluctance. Gould felt that some areas were inferior and described the putto on the extreme left by the clavichord in 'Unfaithfulness' (Plate 2) as 'coarsely modelled' when compared with the other putto.[7] He was, however, distrustful of dividing responsibility for the pictures between the artist and his studio, and rightly opposed to the categorical distinctions between paintings 'wholly' by the artist (NG 1318 and 1324) and others by the studio such as are found in earlier catalogues.[8] It should be added that both the condition of parts of the pictures and the way they are displayed would inhibit assessments of quality. Slight abrasion of the globe in 'Happy Union' diminishes its rotundity. And anatomical infelicities in the nude woman enthroned upon this globe might seem brilliantly calculated were the painting to be exhibited on a ceiling.

Technique and materials

Since Veronese's four canvases constitute a series (Plates 2–5), it might be expected that the painting technique would show close similarities from one painting to another; this is born out in fact. Three of the series (NG 1324–6) were studied during cleaning in 1982;[9] 'Unfaithfulness' (NG 1318) was examined subsequently. Initial results of pigment and layer structure analysis acquired in the early 1980s using microscopical methods,[10] LMA,[11] XRD and preliminary media analyses by GC have been supplemented more recently with SEM–EDX studies and HPLC identification of lake pigment dyestuffs, particularly of the reds, using techniques described on pp. 59–63 of this *Bulletin*. New organic analytical results for glazes suspected to be of the 'copper resinate' type have been obtained by Jennifer Pilc using FTIR,[12] a method that had not been available during the earlier studies. A summary of the results is presented in the Table for ease of comparison between the four compositions.

It is often suggested that these canvas paintings were painted in a technique, if not wholly

Fig. 1 Suggested arrangement of Veronese's *Allegories* as ceiling decoration.

simulating the appearance of *buon fresco* or *fresco secco*, then at least of the general tonality of fresco painting, for which Veronese was justifiably admired by this late stage of his career.[13] Working on canvas in this way would reproduce the effects attainable in fresco in paintings which could be transported to their eventual setting with relative ease. However, the painting techniques of the Allegories, as revealed by examination of samples, show more complex intentions on Veronese's part: in the use of glazes – which are not a fundamental method of fresco painting and particularly not of *buon fresco* – and in the general construction of colour in the four paintings, which rests on an unexpectedly rich and varied palette.

One difficulty in interpreting Veronese's conception for this group of compositions is the extent to which the colours have changed. The likely loss of a once more powerful blue in the skies is perhaps most immediately striking, but as has been noted in an earlier account of one of the compositions, 'Respect', there are other colour changes, equally dramatic and distorting, which cannot be assessed by casual observation. The apparently inconsistent behaviour of the green glazes, some of which are well preserved whereas others are not, is one such example.[14]

Fig. 2 Preparatory drawings for Veronese's *Allegories*. Pen and brown ink with brown wash, 32.4 × 22.2 cm. New York, The Metropolitan Museum of Art (Harry G. Sperling Fund, no. 1975.150).

Also, there is evidence for fading in the reds where the paint layers contain red lake (dyestuff) pigments.[15] In addition to these changes which result from alterations to pigments, there are the effects of wearing in the paint layers and the visual consequences of old, harsh relining methods used for canvases which are not only fragile but sensitive to darkening as a result of their gesso ground structures. Some of these changes serve to render the pictures darker overall; others, particularly fading of pigments, result in a general lightening of tone.

Rearick has suggested that the greyish appearance of the skies was a deliberate method of Veronese's to decrease perspectival depth in compositions designed to be seen from below; he comments on the tonality of the *Allegories*: 'Colour is muted to a restrained harmony of earth tones against a pallid sky of a slightly lilac hue, an unusual device and often used by Paolo in 1550 to reduce the suggestion of deep, empty space and focus attention on the foreground figures.'[16] But it is quite clear also that the smalt pigment used in all four paintings for the sky has suffered loss of colour,

Fig. 3 Paolo Veronese, *Allegory of Love, III* ('Respect') (NG 1325). Detail showing adjustment of the outline of the head during the course of execution.

since a proportion of individual pigment particles show, under the microscope, a blue core and a decolorised periphery, characteristic of progressive loss of colour as the cobalt content is leached from the outer edges of the particles.[17] Further, where smalt is used on its own in oil, and is therefore more vulnerable to loss of colour, as in, for example, the underlayers for the cupid's azurite-containing wing in 'Scorn', decolorisation of the smalt is total and only the yellow-brown colour of the dried oil medium is evident in the paint layer and in samples under the microscope.

Firm evidence for other colour changes comes from examination of thin paint cross-sections by transmitted light. These changes include surface embrownment of green copper-containing glazes, particularly that used for the brocade design covering the central square column in 'Respect'[18] (see Plate 4), when compared with constitutionally similar glazes protected on canvas edges turned over the stretcher. Similarly, a red lake glaze from the curtain, also in 'Respect', which had been protected from light under old patches of repaint, proved deeper in colour than the surrounding, exposed paint.

The basic structure of the four pictures follows many of the standard Venetian methods for painting on canvas.[19] Although they were painted fairly late in the sixteenth century, Veronese retained the technique of applying thin gesso grounds bound in animal glue to the canvases. These are plain-weave (tabby) linen, medium in weight with average thread counts of 13 by 13 threads/cm (measured on the X-ray photographs; see, for example, Fig. 4). The canvases are fairly accurately square in format and although the dimensions now differ from one another by a few centimetres, varying amounts of the painted surfaces are turned over the present stretchers. All four compositions have a horizontal seam joining two widths of canvas roughly along the central axes of the paintings (see Figs. 4 and 5), each strip being close to the maximum standard loom width (roughly one metre) often found for Venetian canvases made up of sewn sections.[20]

Over the gesso in each case is a thin light greyish-brown *imprimitura*, largely composed of lead white lightly tinted with a finely ground black pigment and some correspondingly fine warm brown, probably an earth such as umber. No large-scale or complete drawings for the series are known, although as we have noted the sheet in New York (Fig. 2) shows some ink and wash figure studies for the series.[21] Infra-red photographs of the paintings reveal very little underdrawing in any kind of infra-red absorbing material. However, several cross-sections show a thin layer of a black dry drawing material directly on the *imprimitura* and this is occasionally visible through the paint on top where it is sufficiently thin, as in, for example,

Fig. 4 Paolo Veronese, *Allegory of Love, I* ('Unfaithfulness'), X-ray detail of the right-hand man's head, showing the plain canvas weave and the area of the head held as a reserve. The horizontal seam in the two pieces of canvas is indicated by the arrow.

Fig. 5 Paolo Veronese, *Allegory of Love, IV* ('Happy Union'). Detail of back of the original canvas after removal of the lining canvas, showing the original horizontal seam.

the sloping profile of the tree-trunk to the left in 'Scorn'. Much of the compositional design appears to have been executed by 'drawing' with a brush using dilute dark paint, either of black, a warm dark brown or a reddish brown, depending on the compositional context, perhaps reinforcing an earlier light linear sketch in a dry medium. Very dark paint can be seen to follow the outlines of the figures, for example in the profiles of the man stretching out his arm in 'Respect' and the woman holding the olive branch in 'Happy Union'. The X-ray photographs show areas of the flesh painting usually held in reserve (see Fig. 4), the reserves indicated by this kind of 'drawing' in fluid paint. Drawing in a warmer brown paint is particularly clear in the head and torso of the woman to the left of centre in 'Scorn', while the position of her golden necklace is sketched on to the flesh paint of her upper chest in a thin line of red-brown paint (Plate 1).

Examination of the surfaces of the paintings in the studio and X-ray photographs of sections of the compositions do not show a great number of significant pentimenti[22] – most of the adjustments to the compositions apparently having been made at the brush-drawn stage of design, by shifting and correcting outlines and modifying certain other compositional relationships, mainly in architectural and foliage details. Thereafter the designs seem largely fixed, except in the precise placing of a figure, the edge of a drapery, or of the volume of a figure or an object. A clear example of a modification of this type can be seen in the backwards tilted head of the man in 'Respect' where the surrounding sky has been extended to cover the earlier outline for the crown of the head (Fig. 3); similarly, a patch of red drapery conceals part of the cupid's wing in a minor modification to the design lower down. There are other cases, such as the outline of the dog's head in 'Happy Union'.

The binding media for the paint layers has been identified as linseed oil for some passages, with walnut oil employed in others, but use of the nut oil medium is more restricted. There is no clear pattern in the division of the two drying oils in Veronese's practice generally[23] and although walnut oil, believed to yellow less with age, was detected only in light-coloured areas, for example in white and in pale yellow drapery passages in 'Respect' and 'Happy Union', other white and light-coloured paints were found to contain linseed oil as the binder. The results of medium analyses of the *Allegories* have been reported in earlier issues of the *Bulletin*,[24] but they are re-summarised in the Table here for convenience.

Veronese's method of painting for the *Allegories* is bold, broad and free in its handling: an approach consistent with compositions planned to be seen from a distance. Even so there are brilliant touches executed on a small scale – highlights on jewellery, hair and dress – which can be appreciated only at close quarters, but presumably Veronese found these demonstrations of his highly developed painterly skills irresistible. The flesh paints show very clearly the broad nature of the technique. They are most often worked up in three incompletely blended values of shadow, middle tone and highlight. Vermilion provides the principal red component for these mixed paints and a variety of earths is incorporated to impart darker and browner hues (Plate 6). Green pigment, generally an olive-coloured variety of *terra verde*, occurs in the cooler, greener shadows of flesh, particularly where the paint is intended to have a translucent quality. The rather lean, dragged brushstrokes of desiccated looking lighter passages which contain a high proportion of white or pale yellow – a common consistency of the paint in Veronese's large later works on canvas – is the tonal aspect that most strongly recalls the look of fresco. Set against these areas, however, are the more saturated glaze-like parts of the compositions, finished in the powerful cold dark greens of 'copper resinate' glaze and turbid-looking red semi-glazing paints, which combine the translucency and colour intensity of deep red lakes with the body and density of vermilion.

The four *Allegories of Love* show much of the richness of palette familiar in Venetian painting and the wide colour range of desirable and valuable materials available to painters. Lapis lazuli ultramarine, frequently employed on a grand and lavish scale in Venice, however, is not found here, but in Veronese's work this clearly does not relate to the importance of the commission or the client.[25] Other than the smalt of the skies, blue is rarely used except for some natural azurite, laid over smalt, for the wings of the cupids both in 'Respect' and 'Scorn' and as a more widespread component of the mixed green paints employed for foliage, particularly that in 'Unfaithfulness'.

A generous use of and reliance on red lake pigments is also a characteristic of Venetian painting; in the *Allegories* the deep purple-red glazes have been identified as based on the dyestuff extracted from cochineal (see p. 63 and p. 71 of this *Bulletin*). Although no other red lake type was detected, Veronese has constructed a considerable colour range in the reds by superimposing red glazes over pink or red underlayers consisting of white, red lake and vermilion in varying combinations and proportions, occasionally adding red lead to widen the colour range further. He has also incorporated vermilion into the red lake glazes, producing hotter, more orange-toned paints. The variation in colour and density in the reds is seen to best effect in the draperies surrounding the recumbent woman in 'Respect' (see Plate 7) and in the contrast between the hanging drapery to the right and the pinkish-red costume of the man to the left in 'Unfaithfulness'.

Plate 2 Paolo Veronese, *Allegory of Love, I* ('Unfaithfulness')
(NG 1318), 1570s. Canvas, 189.9 × 189.9 cm.

Plate 3 Paolo Veronese, *Allegory of Love, II* ('Scorn')
(NG 1324), 1570s. Canvas, 186.6 × 188.5 cm.

Ground Gesso[1] + light grey-brown *imprimitura*[2]

Medium Linseed oil: two samples (white sheet; foliage)

Sky Smalt[3] + white[4]

Flesh paints Pink of woman's back: vermilion + white
Greenish shadow: white + *terra verde*[5] (black, earths, red lead)
Darker flesh of right-hand man's neck: vermilion, red lake, red lead[6] (black, earths)
Mid-tone, left-hand cupid: lead white + haematite[7] over mixed underlayer

Red draperies Deep red shadow on left-hand man's sleeve: red lake[8] + vermilion over red lake + white
Mid-tone red of left-hand man's sleeve: red lake[8] + vermilion over vermilion + white
Shadow of drapery, right-hand side: red lake + vermilion
Mid-tone of drapery, right-hand side: scumble of red lake + vermilion over red lake + white

Green draperies Dark bluish-green drapery beneath woman: azurite over smalt[9] + white

Yellow and orange draperies Yellow embroidery highlight on left-hand man's coat: lead-tin yellow (II)[10]
Darker yellow embroidery highlight: lead-tin yellow (II)[10]
Yellow-brown lacing on right-hand man's tunic: lead-tin yellow (II)[11] + vermilion (red lead)
Deep lemon yellow light of right-hand man's drapery: lead-tin yellow (I)[12]
Yellow-brown shadow of right-hand man's drapery: white, lead-tin yellow (I) + earths
Brightest orange of right-hand man's tunic: orpiment[13] + realgar[14]
Red-brown shadow on right-hand man's tunic: orpiment, vermilion, red lake (earths, black)
Red-brown lacing on tunic: orpiment + realgar

White and grey draperies Pure white of drapery beneath woman: lead white
Mid-grey shadow on drapery: carbon black[15] + white (red lead)
Darkest grey-black shadow on drapery: scumble of black over dark grey

Foliage Mid-yellow green highlight on leaf: browned green glaze (verdigris/'copper resinate')[16] over lead-tin yellow + azurite
Solid mid-green of leaf: lead-tin yellow + *terra verde* (yellow lake, verdigris)
Dark brownish-green leaf, left-hand side: verdigris + yellow lake (*terra verde*)
Dark translucent brown foliage, centre, left: verdigris/'copper resinate' (discoloured) over brown underlayer containing earths

Ground Gesso[1] + light grey-brown *imprimitura*[2]

Medium Linseed oil (?): four samples (sky; pale pink of woman's sash; orange-brown border; foliage)

Sky Smalt[3] + white[4]

Flesh paints Mid-pink of man's finger: vermilion + white over darker underlayers
Brownish shadow on cupid's arm: white with red lake, haematite (black, *terra verde*)

Red draperies None

Green draperies Bright green of woman's drapery, left-hand edge: verdigris/'copper resinate'[16] glaze over verdigris, malachite + white

Yellow and orange draperies Brightest yellow highlight on man's drapery: lead-tin yellow (I)[12]
Yellow over orange of drapery, right-hand side: lead-tin yellow (I) highlight over red lead[6] underlayer (see Plate 9)
Lighter orange drapery, right-hand side: lead-tin yellow + red lead
Deepest red-brown of drapery, right-hand side: intense red-brown earth[17]

White and grey draperies Grey-blue stripe on woman's dress: azurite + red lake scumble over light grey comprising white, fine black and smalt
Pure white of same dress: lead white

Foliage Dull yellow-green on right-hand turnover: azurite + earths
Brown tree-trunk, left-hand turnover: browned green glaze[18] over lead-tin yellow + verdigris

Notes to the Table

Pigments cited in brackets are minor proportions of the paint layer.
Media results are given in ref. 24.

1. Calcium sulphate identified by EDX; SEM micrographs show tabular texture characteristic of gypsum (calcium sulphate dihydrate). Insufficient material was available for confirmation as gypsum by XRD.
2. The *imprimitura* layer entirely covers the gesso ground in each painting. It is composed principally of lead white with a little fine black and warm brown (umber). Staining tests indicate an oil binder.
3. Smalt (blue potash glass containing cobalt) confirmed by EDX (Si, K, Co; also As, Fe). Decolorised smalt had a lower cobalt content than that in the blue particles.
4. Lead white (basic lead carbonate) containing some neutral carbonate was the only white pigment detected in the paint layers. Confirmed by XRD in several cases (JCPDS file No.13–131).
5. Earth pigment containing glauconite or celadonite. Identification by microscopy and EDX (K, Si, Al, Fe, Mg).
6. Red lead refers to lead tetroxide (Pb_3O_4) or *minium*.
7. Crystalline dark red-brown iron oxide pigment; microscopically characteristic.
8. Dyestuff identified by HPLC as derived from cochineal, probably the New World insect (Dactylopius coccus Costa); see also p. 71 of this *Bulletin*. EDX

Plate 4 Paolo Veronese, *Allegory of Love, III* ('Respect') (NG 1325), 1570s. Canvas, 186.1 × 194.3 cm.

Plate 5 Paolo Veronese, *Allegory of Love, IV* ('Happy Union') (NG 1326), 1570s. Canvas, 187.4 × 186.7 cm.

<u>Ground</u> Gesso[1] + light grey-brown *imprimitura*[2]

<u>Medium</u> Linseed oil: three samples (red curtain, right; deep green of sash; browned green brocade). Walnut oil: two samples (white of sheet; pale yellow drapery)

<u>Sky</u> Smalt[3] + white[4]

<u>Flesh paints</u> Shadow of man's forearm: earths, red lake, black, brown *terra verde* (lead-tin yellow [II][11])
Mid-tone of forearm: vermilion, white, brown, black
Lightest tone on forearm: white, vermilion (earths, black)

<u>Red draperies</u> Glazed area of curtain, right: red lake[8] (black)
Browner red of curtain: thin red lake[8] + vermilion over red lake (white)
Mauver pink of curtain: thick red lake glaze over red lake and white underlayer
Denser red of curtain: vermilion + red lake + white over red lake + white
Highlight on drapery on which woman is lying: red lake + vermilion over red lake, vermilion and white. Red lake (red lead, black) underneath (see Plate 7)

<u>Green draperies</u> Moss green of drapery on man's chest: 'copper resinate'/verdigris glaze over white
Darker green drapery at shoulder: 'copper resinate'/verdigris over two layers of verdigris + white
Darkest shadow of drapery near chin: 'copper resinate'/verdigris over two layers of verdigris + white
Brown background to brocade textile on column: lead-tin yellow, earths, black over grey-brown underlayer
Deep brown glaze-like brocade background: 'copper resinate'/verdigris glaze, browned at surface over dark grey-brown underlayer
Thin area of glaze design: 'copper resinate'/verdigris glaze, heavily discoloured

<u>Yellow and orange draperies</u> Brightest yellow of skirt of tunic: lead-tin yellow (II) + white
Brownish yellow of lining: lead-tin yellow (II),[11] white (umber[19])

<u>White and grey draperies</u> White of sheet: lead white

<u>Ground</u> Gesso[1] + light grey-brown *imprimitura*[2]

<u>Medium</u> Linseed oil: five samples (bright green glaze on man's tunic; white of dog; bright yellow cloak; orange drapery left; red glaze on woman's dress). Walnut oil: one sample (pale yellow drapery)

<u>Sky</u> Smalt[3] + white[4]

<u>Flesh paints</u> Shadow of palm of man's hand: earths, vermilion, white (black, *terra verde*) (see Plate 6)
Pinkish mid-tone of finger: white, vermilion (red lake, red lead)
Highlight on man's forearm: white (translucent brown, vermilion)

<u>Red draperies</u> Red glaze from brocade dress: red lake[8] (black, white)
Pink of dress: red lake + white in two layers

<u>Green draperies</u> Yellow-green highlights of woman's drapery, left: lead-tin yellow (I) (white, red lead, verdigris) with thin, partially browned glaze. Red lake layer with black beneath
Deep green of man's sleeve: 'copper resinate'/verdigris glaze with some white over solid green of verdigris + white (see Plate 8)
Darker green of sleeve: 'copper resinate'/verdigris glaze,[18] browned at surface
Criss-cross pattern on man's tunic: thin, severely browned green glaze over lead-tin yellow + verdigris underlayer

<u>Yellow and orange draperies</u> Brightest yellow of man's cloak: lead-tin yellow (II)[10] + white
Yellow brocade highlight on woman's dress: lead-tin yellow (II)[10] + white (see Plate 10)
Brightest orange: orpiment[13] over realgar[14]
Brownish orange of drapery on stone globe: orpiment, realgar, red lake
Deep orange drapery on stone globe: pararealgar[20]

<u>White and grey draperies</u> None

<u>Foliage</u> Mid-green of olive leaf: verdigris, white + earths with 'copper resinate'/verdigris glaze, rather browned

analysis of the red lake substrates shows the presence of Al, Ca, Si, K.
9. The smalt, mixed with white and protected from light beneath an upper paint layer, is relatively undiscoloured here.
10. Lead-tin yellow (II) has the composition Pb(Sn,Si)O$_3$, cubic in structure, confirmed by XRD (see ref. 29).
11. Individual pigment particles in cross-sections confirmed as lead-tin yellow (II) by EDX (Pb, Sn, Si) guided by back-scattered electron images in the SEM (see ref. 30).
12. Lead-tin yellow (I) has the composition Pb$_2$SnO$_4$, tetragonal in structure, confirmed by XRD (see ref. 31 and JCPDS file Nos. 11-233 and 24-589).
13. Orpiment, yellow arsenic(III) sulphide (As$_2$S$_3$), confirmed by EDX (As, S) and XRD (JCPDS file No. 19-84). The particle form in some specimens indicated the mineral variety, showing characteristic large striated lemon-yellow flakes, with a waxy sheen.
14. Realgar, orange-red arsenic(II) sulphide (AsS), confirmed by EDX (As, S) and XRD (JCPDS file No. 41-1494). See also note 20 below.
15. Fine, slightly rounded and faceted shiny particles suggest a vegetable black pigment, not wood charcoal.

16. In many of the green glazes, undissolved or unreacted verdigris particles are detectable under the microscope; a number of particle types are present (see ref. 32). FTIR–microscopy of several samples indicated verdigris and oil with added resin, but weaker resin bands than true 'copper resinates'. EDX analysis in all cases, including browned surface glazes, showed a high copper content; in certain cases chloride was also detected in the greens and may result from the method of preparation for verdigris (see ref. 33). Lead (as added lead white) is a common component of the more turbid semiglazes.
17. This area contains a particularly strongly coloured pure red-brown natural earth pigment of very uniform tone and grain size. EDX showed Fe, Si, Ca (low Al).
18. True 'copper resinate' confirmed by the detection by GC–MS of pine-resin components derived from dehydroabietic acid in the glaze (see refs. 24 and 34).
19. Iron and manganese detected by EDX.
20. Strongly coloured orange-yellow fine-grained pigment, identified as pararealgar by XRD (JCPDS file No. 33-127) (see ref. 35).

41

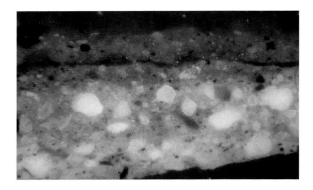

Plate 6 'Happy Union' (NG 1326). Cross-section from shadow value of the palm of the man's outstretched hand, consisting of a scumble of earths with black, over a mixture of earth pigments, vermilion and white, and small quantities of *terra verde* and black. The greyish-brown *imprimitura* is visible beneath. Original magnification 275 ×; actual magnification 230 ×.

Plate 7 'Respect' (NG 1325). Cross-section from highlight of red drapery on which woman is lying, comprising red lake and vermilion over a layer of red lake, vermilion and white. A purer red lake layer is visible beneath. The *imprimitura* and discoloured gesso are also visible. Original magnification 255 ×; actual magnification 215 ×.

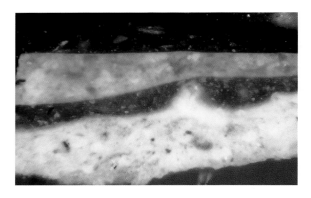

Plate 8 'Happy Union' (NG 1326). Cross-section from deepest green of man's sleeve, showing a surface 'copper resinate'/verdigris type glaze over a solid underpaint of verdigris and white. A more saturated glaze-like green layer is present beneath. Original magnification 240 ×; actual magnification 210 ×.

Plate 9 'Scorn' (NG 1324). Cross-section from yellow highlight over orange of man's drapery, consisting of lead-tin yellow ('type I') on top of a red lead (lead tetroxide) underlayer. Layers containing earth pigments are present beneath. Original magnification 220 ×; actual magnification 185 ×.

Plate 10 (*right*) 'Happy Union' (NG 1326). Cross-section from yellow brocade highlight on woman's pink dress, made up of of lead-tin yellow ('type II') combined with lead white. Layers containing red lake and red lake with white form the underlying paint of the dress. Original magnification 230 ×; actual magnification 195 ×.

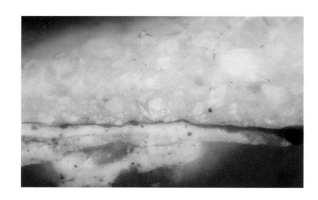

The pictures make significant use of richly applied green glazes based on copper-containing pigments, in some cases true 'copper resinate' in which the resinous content has been confirmed by analysis;[26] in other areas, glaze-like paints contain verdigris as the colouring matter, apparently without added resin. These deep saturated greens, often very well preserved in Veronese's work, are generally applied over underlayers which have a significant influence on the final colour (Plate 8) and, it has been noted in an earlier account of the glazes in 'Respect', on the state of their preservation.[27] The strongest, brightest greens result from glazes applied over solid underpaints of lead white and lead-tin yellow combined with verdigris or verdigris and malachite mixtures as in, for example, the man's deep green sash and cape in 'Respect'. The foliage paints, on the other hand, range from dull greens to browner tones and are constructed using more variable methods. They are rather thinly painted in comparison to the draperies and incorporate a wider range of pigments, including azurite, earths, yellow lakes and black, as well as malachite, verdigris and translucent copper-containing greens, these final glazes sometimes showing signs of discoloration to brown.

As in the reds there is also a remarkable variation in tonal range in the dense yellows and orange colours, principally in the drapery paints (Plates 9 and 10). For these, Veronese exploits an unusually broad selection of pigments, and this must be for their particular colour qualities. Both types of the two varieties of lead-tin yellow occur,[28] which differ in their colour from the light primrose yellow of pure 'type I' to the much deeper, rather more golden slightly acid hue associated with 'type II'. Golden-yellow mineral orpiment and mineral realgar, ranging from orange to red-brown, are used, and also red lead (lead tetroxide, *minium*), brick red in colour, as well as combinations of these pigments with vermilion, red lake, earths and others (see Table).

The overall effects in the pictures, although they are simply and broadly constructed, are as rich and varied as any in Veronese's career, and show all the advantages in materials that the painters in Venice commanded and could pass on to their patrons.

The Vision of Saint Helena

Of all the paintings by Veronese in the National Gallery, that of *The Vision of Saint Helena* (Plate 11) is certainly the one which has received least scholarly attention. The unusual subject can also be seen in a canvas by the artist now in the Pinacoteca of the Vatican,[36] but comparison between these two works underlines two anomalous features of the National Gallery's picture — the vanishing point (and hence implied viewing position), which is below the lower edge, and the asymmetry of the composition. The painting was surely designed to be seen from below and intended as one of a pair of paintings, hanging to the right of another. It is surprising that it seems never previously to have been proposed in print that it was very probably made as one of the shutters for an organ. Such shutters painted on canvas were common in north-east Italy in the late fifteenth century and throughout the sixteenth. Many survive, although relatively few of them actually perform their original function. Some are considerably larger — for example those by Veronese which remain in S. Sebastiano in Venice or those now in the Galleria Estense, Modena, which were originally made by him for S. Geminiano, Venice[37] — but the size of the *Saint Helena* is not very different from that of the *Annunciation* formerly in the church of the Misericordia and now in the Museo Civico, Padua (a painting once frequently given to Veronese but now acknowledged as the work of Giambattista Zelotti).[38]

Although the imagery painted on these shutters was varied, often relating to principal saints venerated within the church, it does sometimes have some relationship to the music performed on the organ which they protected. It is possible that another dreaming saint would have faced Saint Helena and that both would have been invisible when the organ was revealed — for the music could have been incompatible with their slumber. It is not unusual for such shutters to include architectural features depicted as if seen from below, as in the *Annunciation* mentioned above or, still more strikingly, the *David calming the Madness of Paul*, also by Zelotti and also in Padua.[39]

Gould's catalogue entry on the painting is mainly concerned with the artist's dependence

Plate 11 Paolo Veronese, *The Vision of Saint Helena* (NG 1041), *c.*1470–80. Canvas, 197.5 × 115.6 cm.

upon an engraving by a follower of Marcantonio Raimondi (Fig. 6), which derives from an invention of Raphael's recorded in a beautiful drawing in the Uffizi which Gould believed to be by Parmigianino.[40] Gould added that 'a relatively early dating' might be supported by the 'fact' that 'Veronese reacted as a young man to the Central Italian influences with which he would have come into contact at Mantua but seems already to have become impervious to them by the time of his visit to Rome'[41] (a visit was recorded by Ridolfi, who claimed that it was made in company with Girolamo Grimani who is known to have been in Rome in 1555, 1560

and 1566).[42] The truth is, however, that such a direct borrowing is unusual in Veronese's art at any date and that neither the colouring nor the technique of this painting can be associated with the artist's early work. Most scholars prefer a date in the 1570s.[43]

Technique and materials

Veronese's *Vision of Saint Helena* is painted on a plain weave canvas made from two pieces, a narrow strip (*c.* 15 cm wide) joined to a larger piece just over a metre in width which, from measurements on other Venetian paintings, appears to be the standard loom width available in Venice at this time.[44] The canvas has been prepared with a thin gesso ground; as in many of Veronese's larger paintings, there is no *imprimitura*. The gesso consists of the dihydrate form of calcium sulphate,[45] probably not as raw gypsum but as rehydrated burnt gypsum (*gesso sottile*).[46] This is a practice retained from the method of preparation of earlier Venetian panels, where the ground often consists entirely of *gesso sottile*.[47] Some very sketchy drawing indicating the main forms, particularly in the drapery of Saint Helena, is visible in the infrared photograph. The photograph also reveals the only major change in the composition: the cross was originally placed at a different angle.

Like the *Allegories of Love* series, *The Vision of Saint Helena* is a painting which invites comparison with fresco because of its strikingly cool and grey tonality. The overall appearance is heavily influenced by the choice of blue pigment for the large area of sky; smalt has been used[48] and has now deteriorated to a pale yellowish-grey colour.[49]

Saint Helena's dress is very loosely painted, with broad strokes, perhaps a technical indication that it was intended for a location where it would be seen at a distance, supporting the suggestion made above that it was an organ shutter. Similarly, the *Allegories* were painted with a broad and economical technique, appropriate for their location on a ceiling, but they are more carefully executed than Saint Helena – the attention to details on jewellery and dress has already been mentioned. The comparison perhaps suggests that the broad technique of *The Vision of Saint Helena* is a result of the unimportance with which Veronese regarded the commission (certainly not equal to the

Allegories), rather than its location. The salmon-pink mid-tones of her overdress are a mixture of lead white and vermilion (Plate 12).[50] The shadows are created by strokes of red lake of a rather purple hue. Her skirt and collar are mustard yellow, with shadows marked by the same red lake-containing paint used in the overdress.

The orange cloth on which Saint Helena sits, and which is draped over the window sill, is painted with the bright yellow mineral orpiment.[51] It is used alone, not mixed, consistent with its reputation for incompatibility with many pigments often mentioned in treatises on painting technique.[52] The brownish shadows are mixtures of red, yellow and brown earth pigments. The lightest highlights are lead white and lead-tin yellow of the 'type II' form,[53] so far found only in Venetian paintings in the sixteenth century;[54] its warmer yellow colour relative to the 'type I' form is evident in this painting, and here it has a distinctive large and angular particle form (Plate 13).[55]

Fig. 6 Follower of Marcantonio Raimondi, *Pensive Woman*. Engraving, 15 × 93 cm. London, British Museum.

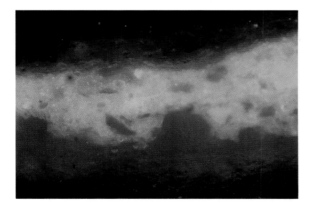

Plate 12 *The Vision of Saint Helena* (NG 1041). Cross-section of the salmon-pink mid-tone of Saint Helena's dress. A thin layer of red lake lies on the gesso ground, over which is a lighter pink layer of red lake and lead white. The uppermost salmon-pink paint is a mixture of lead white, red lake and vermilion. Original magnification 750 ×; actual magnification 620 ×.

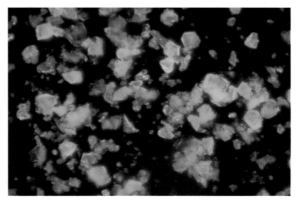

Plate 13 *The Vision of Saint Helena* (NG 1041). Dispersed sample of lead-tin yellow 'type II', mixed with some lead white, from a highlight of the yellow drapery on which Saint Helena sits. The yellow pigment particles are unusually large, with a distinctive glassy appearance. Original magnification 275 ×; actual magnification 230 ×.

The Adoration of the Kings

The four *Allegories* and *The Vision of Saint Helena* are regarded, on stylistic and other grounds, as belonging to the 1570s, but the *Adoration of the Kings* (Plate 14) is a rare example of a painting by Veronese which is actually inscribed with a date – M.D. LXXIII, for 1573 – on the lowest stone step in the right foreground. The painting was made for the church of S. Silvestro in Venice where it is often said to have served as the high altarpiece, but where it evidently hung on the left and, it seems, between two altars.[56] When this church was remodelled in the first half of the last century it transpired that the larger paintings, such as this one, which had been stored nearby no longer fitted.[57] Such a confusion is rather unconvincing and is likely to have been an excuse to sell this and other pictures with impunity, replacing them with works more congenial to nineteenth-century piety and using the funds raised by the sale for the remodelling. The painting's acquisition by the Gallery in 1855 was regarded as a considerable coup since the Rothschilds in Paris also had their eye on it.[58] One may, however, suspect that there was some disappointment with it, otherwise the Gallery would not have devoted so much effort and so many funds to the acquisition of the *Family of Darius* two years later. The two paintings were, of course, different in type, the *Adoration* made for a church and resembling an altarpiece. But the Gallery already possessed a Veronese altarpiece (*The Consecration of Saint Nicholas* – acquired in 1826) and the *Adoration* probably appealed because it involved ceremonial movement in front of a screen of classical architecture, with majestic figures, richly attired and accompanied by a large and lively retinue of animals and servants. In other words, it was precisely the sort of composition for which Veronese was most admired in his refectory and palace decorations; it may be that a close acquaintance with a Veronese of this type helped to stimulate enthusiasm for the *Family of Darius*, for despite the high quality of the *Adoration* it is a painting in which the extensive participation of Veronese's large and well-co-ordinated workshop may be discerned. Gould, in his catalogue entry for the picture, noted that 1573 was the year in which Veronese also completed and inscribed *The Last Supper* for the Dominican refectory of SS. Giovanni e Paolo (which after his appearance before the Inquisition was converted to *The Feast in the House of Levi*), *The Madonna of the Rosary*, a large altarpiece for S. Pietro Martire, Murano, and *A Trinity with Saints Peter and Paul* for S. Croce, Vicenza.[59] Studio assistance is therefore hardly surprising. But while such assistance has long been recognised, it has not been recognised in the same places. For example, Gould considered that Veronese's 'own touch is unmistakable' in the Madonna and Child,[60] but Morelli, and following him Richter, considered, justly, that the painting included much that was reminiscent of the family and followers of Jacopo Bassano,[61] and surely this is notably true of the Virgin's features.

The composition is similar to the altarpiece with the same subject which Veronese painted for the Cogoli Chapel in S. Corona in his native Verona which is however smaller in size and less square in format.[62] This chapel is known to have been completed in the years following 1573, so the S.Corona altarpiece is likely to be later than the National Gallery painting which was dated in that year. Moreover, its composition looks as if it was adapted, with an uncomfortable degree of compression, from that of the larger painting. A sheet of preparatory figure studies in the Teylers Museum, Haarlem, also seems to show Veronese working out the composition for the S. Silvestro painting rather than that for S. Corona, but he seems to have reverted in his composition for the latter to at least one idea abandoned in the former.[63] Paradoxically, however, the painting in Verona is not only superior in condition but more clearly autograph in execution. The very completeness and assurance of the design of the larger altarpiece, which may reflect the prominence of the commission, may also have been necessary if the execution was to have been delegated efficiently. No pentimenti are apparent in it like those in the *Family of Darius*.

Technique and materials
The canvas of *The Adoration of the Kings* is made from three pieces, each just over a metre wide, joined by two horizontal seams.[64] It has a plain (tabby) weave and is prepared with a thin white ground composed of calcium

Plate 14 Paolo Veronese, *The Adoration of the Kings* (NG 268), 1573. Canvas, 355.6 × 320 cm.

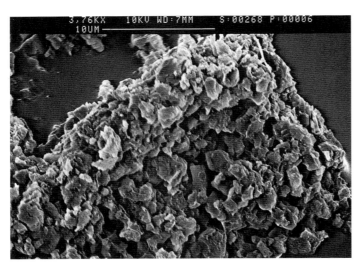

Fig. 7 *The Adoration of the Kings* (NG 268). Secondary electron image of the ground in the scanning electron microscope. The particles of calcium carbonate are relatively small and uniform; there are no coccoliths such as are found in natural chalk.

carbonate (bound in glue), together with a small proportion of silicaceous minerals which are probably impurities associated with calcium carbonate.[65] This is extremely unusual for a sixteenth-century Venetian painting where gesso (calcium sulphate) is almost invariably found; very occasionally a ground consisting of a mixture of gypsum and calcite has been identified.[66] The watertight provenance of *The Adoration of the Kings* rules out any possibility that it was not painted in Italy. In most Northern European paintings, where calcium carbonate grounds are standard, they contain natural chalk, identifiable by the presence of coccoliths, the fossil remains of unicellular algae from which chalk originates. They are visible at high magnification in the scanning electron microscope, but were not found in the ground on *The Adoration of the Kings*; the calcium carbonate must have some other origin.

Calcium carbonate exists in several polymorphic forms; in this case it has the calcite (rhombohedral) crystal structure, the most common form in nature, occurring as natural chalk, limestone and marble.[67] Veronese would probably have had limestone in his studio for fresco – we know that he was painting a fresco on the façade of the Palazzo Erizzo around this time.[68] Marble was also used in fresco painting, but it is usually coarse; the particles in this ground are relatively small (Fig. 7).[69] Limestone seems the most likely origin of the calcium carbonate;[70] it was perhaps used accidentally, or the large number of paintings being produced may have resulted in a shortage of gypsum for grounds. There is no *imprimitura*, the composition was painted directly on the ground. The surviving drawings are studies of figure groups rather than sketches of the entire composition.[71] Some drawing in a dry black material such as chalk or charcoal can be seen on the painting where the paint is thin, particularly in areas of flesh such as the faces of the principal figures.

The sky is painted with azurite, giving the painting a very different appearance from the cool tones of *The Allegories of Love*, where the sky consists of greyish discoloured smalt. The Virgin's blue cloak is also painted with azurite; in fact, azurite is the only blue pigment in the painting. It is used again to achieve a purple-grey paint in the lining of the central king's coat, where it is mixed with a little red lake

Balthasar's green coat is well preserved in colour; there is no sign of brown discoloured 'copper resinate' glazes. The underlayers contain coarse natural malachite, with some azurite and yellow.[72] Verdigris is used only in the more transparent upper layers of dark green, applied to indicate shadows in the drapery. The copper green pigments are mixed with large particles of lead-tin yellow of the 'type II' form (Plate 15), very similar in appearance to the lead-tin yellow in *The Family of Darius before Alexander*.[73]

The foliage which overlaps the sky near the top of the painting is a rather brownish green. The paint contains verdigris, some malachite, yellow earth and black. Although the brownish colour might lead to the suspicion that, as in *The Allegories of Love*, a 'copper resinate' type glaze may have discoloured, this complicated mixture suggests that the paint was never intended to be a pure bright green.[74]

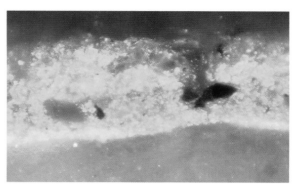

Plate 15 *The Adoration of the Kings* (NG 268). Cross-section of a shadow in Balthasar's green cloak. There are three green paint layers above the calcium carbonate ground in this sample. The lower lighter green layers contain large particles of natural malachite and lead-tin yellow 'type II', with small amounts of azurite and lead white. The uppermost dark green paint marks the shadow and contains verdigris and a little lead-tin yellow. Original magnification 220 ×, actual magnification 170 ×.

Plate 16 *The Adoration of the Kings* (NG 268). Orange sleeve of the man leaning over the cow in the centre of the painting. The cross-section shows several layers of paint containing yellow pararealgar (arsenic[II] sulphide) and some vermilion. Original magnification 750 ×; actual magnification 590 ×.

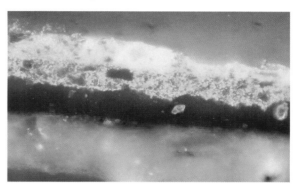

Plate 17 *The Adoration of the Kings* (NG 268). Cross-section through the red brocade cloak of the kneeling king. A layer of red lake, intense in colour, lies directly on the ground. A more opaque red paint of vermilion and red lake forms the brocade pattern, and a further lighter layer (vermilion, lead white, red lake) indicates the highlight. Original magnification 600 ×; actual magnification 470 ×.

Lead-tin yellow of the 'type II' form and of large particle size was also found in the highlights of the gold and white brocade coat of the kneeling king nearest the Virgin.[75] The shadows of the yellow pattern representing gold threads are painted with yellow earth.

The orange coat of the man leaning over a cow in the centre of the painting contains a bright yellow mineral pigment, identified by X-ray diffraction as pararealgar (arsenic[II] sulphide), a polymorph of realgar.[76] Pararealgar can be formed as a result of the deterioration of realgar, but the total absence of realgar in the sample argues against this possibility. In addition, in more orange areas of the drapery such as the shadows, the yellow is mixed with vermilion, which also suggests that the paint did not originally contain orange realgar (Plate 16).

Cross-sections from the red brocade coat of the kneeling king next to Balthasar reveal thick layers of red lake directly on the ground (Plate 17). For the lighter pattern of the brocade an opaque paint of vermilion and red lake is used, mixed with lead white in the highlights. Modelling on the coat is achieved with further red lake glazes. Analysis of the red lake by HPLC identified cochineal as the source of the dyestuff, precipitated on to an alumina substrate. More specifically, it is possible to identify the type of cochineal as Polish (Old World)

cochineal;[77] it is interesting that the red lake pigment in *The Allegories of Love* is prepared from New World cochineal,[78] although both would already have been available in Venice in 1573 when *The Adoration of the Kings* was painted.

The duller red-brown robe of a more peripheral figure, the page at the extreme left edge of the painting, has been painted with a red earth pigment mixed with some lead white and black. Some of the particles visible in the cross-section have the distinctive dark red and highly refracting appearance of haematite. The modelling is achieved with red lake glazes, and red lake mixed into the earth-containing paint.

The colours, and the pigments used to achieve them, are as varied as would be

Fig. 8 Paolo Veronese, *Crucifixion*. Black stone, 84 × 38 cm. Signed 'PAVLO'. Padua, Museo Civico.

expected in a painting by a Venetian artist. The materials are very similar to those found in a recent study of the technique of *The Feast in the House of Levi*[79] which was painted in the same year, particularly in the use of malachite, haematite, and lead-tin yellow 'type II'. The most unusual feature of the materials in the *Adoration*, however, must be the calcium carbonate ground, perhaps the only reported example in an Italian painting of the sixteenth century.

Conclusions

A justification for this study of Veronese's paintings in the National Gallery is that the collection includes examples of both his early and late work and also examples of the different types of painting that he undertook. But some indication of the limitations of the sample should be noted. No examples of canvases with relatively small figures have been included. These are not only some of the most exquisite of Veronese's paintings, but most scholars agree that some of them are likely to date from late in his career. Veronese died in 1588 and was certainly active during the 1580s – for example the great altarpiece now in the Musée des Beaux Arts, Dijon, was commissioned in 1586[80] and the high altar of San Pantaleone in the following year[81] – none of the paintings in the National Gallery has been dated so late.

One of the most remarkable of the smaller late paintings by Veronese is the beautiful signed *Crucifixion* (Fig. 8) painted on stone, which is in the Museo Civico, Padua.[82] Here, as in other (later) examples by artists from Verona, much of the picture surface consists simply of the highly polished stone which represents the deep black of the night sky.[83] That in itself is of interest, but so, too, is the idea of painting on a dark ground which this technique necessarily involves. The latter part of Veronese's career coincided with a period of change in painting technique in Italy – experimentation with alternative supports and dark grounds were part of this change. Some of Veronese's late canvas paintings of the Passion, most notably *The Agony in the Garden* in the Brera Gallery in Milan,[84] clearly have such a ground. Nor did the artist favour it only for sombre subjects. One of the most beautiful of his late small canvases, *The Finding of Moses* in the Musée des Beaux-Arts, Lyon, is also painted on a dark ground.[85]

The larger painting of *Mars and Venus* (Fig. 9) in the National Gallery of Scotland, generally regarded as a late work, and by some as a workshop production, is painted on a dark ground but with a dense area of lead white for the radiant nude body of the goddess (Fig. 10), with an effect more dramatic today than the artist is likely to have foreseen.[86]

However routine Veronese's followers and

assistants were as artists, they seem to have participated in the experiments of the artist's last years. Striking testimony to their interest in technical innovation is the large altarpiece of the *Pietà and Saints* the family workshop is known to have supplied to S. Giobbe in Venice which is painted on metal, probably copper – one of the very few altarpieces anywhere painted on such a support.[87]

Even if there are aspects of Veronese's technique which are not represented by the paintings in the National Gallery examined in this article, we can feel sure that the works discussed here are likely to be characteristic of the mainstream of Veronese's work, and, indeed, central to Venetian practice of painting on canvas in general. The National Gallery's Veroneses thus provide norms against which other examples of his painting – and that by other artists working in Venice and the Veneto in the mid-sixteenth century – can be measured.

Notes and References

1. For the inventory taken after 15 February 1637 see C. Gould, *The Sixteenth Century Italian Schools*, National Gallery Catalogues, London 1959 (revised in 1975), p. 329.
2. For the earlier inventory of 1621 – also posthumous because Rudolph died in 1612 – see Gould, cited in note 1, p. 328. Gould regarded it as merely 'a possibility that they had been commissioned by Rudolf'. It is surely a strong probability, for no other pictures of this character and quality seem to have entered the Imperial Collection between Rudolph's death and 1637. The schemes employed on Venetian ceilings are discussed by J. Schulz in *Venetian Painted Ceilings of the Renaissance*, Berkeley and Los Angeles 1968. It may not be generally accepted that the National Gallery's *Allegories* were intended for a ceiling – Gould observed merely that it was 'plausible enough' (p. 328).
3. Full discussions of this drawing are to be found in R. Cocke, *Veronese's Drawings*, London 1984, pp. 184–5, no. 78, and in W.R. Rearick, *The Art of Paolo Veronese*, exhibition catalogue, National Gallery of Art, Washington 1988, no. 62, pp. 125–6.
4. For a brief general survey of Veronese's work for Rudolph see Rearick, cited in note 3, pp. 120–2.
5. Rudolph's marriage to Isabella, eldest daughter of Philip II of Spain (1566–1633), was planned in 1571 but came to nothing. His liaison with Anna Maria Strada, by whom he had six

Fig. 9 Paolo Veronese, *Mars and Venus*. Edinburgh, National Gallery of Scotland.

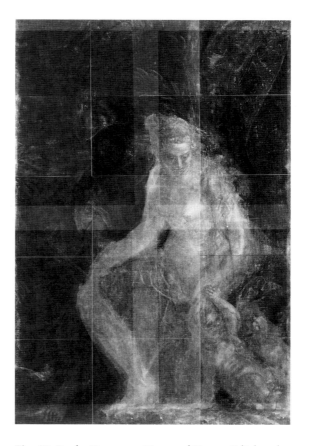

Fig. 10 Paolo Veronese, *Mars and Venus*. Edinburgh, National Gallery of Scotland. X-ray detail of Venus.

children, commenced in 1583 and it is just possible that the union celebrated in these pictures was with her. That might explain some aspects of the subject matter, such as the emphasis on lust, even lust overcome, and the episode of the woman (apparently) shared by two men (Anna Maria was married) which might seem surprising for a bride. And then if these pictures were in a residence of the Emperor's mistress the interval before they were inventoried as part of the Imperial Collection might also be explained. Speculations as to the meanings of the *Allegories* will be found in E. Wind, *Pagan Mysteries in the Renaissance*, Harmondsworth 1967, appendix 8, pp. 272–5; A. Braham, 'Veronese's Allegories of Love', *Burlington Magazine*, 1970, pp. 158–62; M. Royalton-Kisch, 'A New Arrangement for Veronese's Allegories of Love in the National Gallery', *Burlington Magazine*, 1978, pp. 158–62; Rearick, cited in note 3, pp. 126–9.

6. Royalton-Kisch (cited in note 5) first raised the issue of the figures looking out, proposing that they were looking from one picture to another. The suggestion about the heraldic centrepiece is Rearick's (cited in note 3, p. 129). He seems not to have realised that Rudolph never married. Royalton-Kisch was the first to propose in print an arrangement like that found in our figure 1, although his arrangement was slightly different.

7. Gould, cited in note 1, p. 328.

8. Ibid. pp. 328–9 and note 3 on p. 330 citing the catalogue of 1929 and the catalogue for the 1947 exhibition of cleaned pictures.

9. Veronese's *Allegories* had been last cleaned and restored between 1946 and 1950: NG 1318 and 1326 (1946); NG 1324 (1950); NG 1325 (1951).

10. Principally examination of paint cross-sections and thin sections by optical microscopy in reflected and transmitted light.

11. Spectrographic (elemental) analysis with the laser microprobe, now superseded by SEM–EDX analysis. For the earlier method, see A. Roy, 'The Laser Microspectral Analysis of Paint', *National Gallery Technical Bulletin*, 3, 1979, pp. 43–50.

12. For work on green copper-containing glazes, see, for example, J. Pilc and R. White, 'The Application of FTIR-Microscopy to the Analysis of Paint Binders in Easel Paintings', *National Gallery Technical Bulletin*, 16, 1995, p. 78 and p. 82.

13. When taken out of their frames for conservation treatment, thin discontinuous painted borders (*c.* 2cm wide) of red-brown and orange-brown were discovered, roughly marking out the edges on each of the compositions. They were most probably drawn on to the finished paintings as part of a procedure to size the pictures for their eventual architectural settings, since Veronese may well have had to make these calculations at a distance. Cross-sections from these borders and analysis of the materials, including the identification of orpiment and realgar, suggest that they are contemporary with Veronese's paintings, but there is also evidence for reinforcement of these painted outlines in red-brown earth pigment passing over old varnish, representing perhaps minor readjustments to the sizes made during the installation of the pictures, or in preparation for framing as later independent compositions.

14. J. Plesters, A. Roy and D. Bomford, 'Interpretation of the magnified image of paint surfaces and samples in terms of condition and appearance of the picture', in N.S. Brommelle and G. Thomson (eds.), *Science and Technology in the Service of Conservation*, Preprints of the IIC Washington Congress, London 1982, pp. 169–70.

15. Thin cross-sections show fading of red lake dyestuffs in the upper portion of surface glazes; also glaze paints protected from light on turnover edges retain a stronger colour than adjacent exposed paint.

16. See Rearick, cited in note 3, p. 128.

17. A clear example of smalt particles retaining a blue core in a sample from Veronese's *Consecration of Saint Nicholas* (NG 26) is published in the first part of this article. See N. Penny and M. Spring, 'Veronese's Paintings in the National Gallery. Technique and Materials: Part I', *National Gallery Technical Bulletin*, 16, 1995, p. 13, plate 8. For the mechanism of discoloration, see B. Mühlethaler and J. Thissen, 'Smalt' in *Artists' Pigments. A Handbook of Their History and Characteristics*, Vol. 2, ed. A. Roy, 1993, pp. 116–21.

18. Plesters, Roy and Bomford, cited in note 14. For a thin section of browned copper green glaze from 'Respect', see H. Kühn, 'Verdigris and Copper Resinate' in A. Roy (ed), cited in note 17, p. 152.

19. For the essentials of Venetian canvas painting technique, see A. Lucas and J. Plesters, 'Titian's "Bacchus and Ariadne"', *National Gallery Technical Bulletin*, 2, 1978, pp. 25–47; J. Plesters, 'Tintoretto's Paintings in the National Gallery. Part II, Materials and Techniques', *National Gallery Technical Bulletin*, 4, 1980, pp. 32–47; also, L. Lazzarini, 'Il Colore nei Pittori Veneziani tra il 1480 e il 1580', *Bollettino d'Arte, Studi Veneziani, Ricerche di Archivio e di Laboratorio*, Supplemento 5, 1983, pp. 135–44.

20. See Plesters, 1980, cited in note 19, p. 37.

21. This sheet of drawings, dated 1575–6, is reproduced in Rearick, cited in note 3, as Cat. No. 62, p. 125.

22. No complete X-ray mosaics were made of the four *Allegories*, although parts of each were X-rayed in 1981–2.

23. See Part I of this article, Penny and Spring, cited in note 17.

24. For NG 1324, see J. Mills and R. White, 'Analyses of Paint Media', *National Gallery Technical Bulletin*, 5, 1981, pp. 66–7; for NG 1318, 1325 and 1326, see J. Mills and R. White, 'Analyses of Paint Media', *National Gallery Technical Bulletin*, 7, 1983, pp. 66–7.

25. Smalt was also detected in the sky and elsewhere in *The Family of Darius before Alexander* (NG 294), evidently an important commission. See N. Penny and M. Spring, cited in note 17, pp. 16–22. Similarly, a commission from the Holy Roman Emperor, for the *Allegories*, would have been significant in value and status.

26. See J. Mills and R. White, 'Organic Mass-Spectrometry of Art Materials: Work in Progress', *National Gallery Technical Bulletin*, 6, 1982, pp. 10–13.

27. Plesters, Roy and Bomford, cited in note 14.

28. The connection of lead-tin yellow (II) to Venice in the sixteenth century and the occurrence of both varieties of the pigment is commented on by H. Kühn in 'Lead-Tin Yellow', A. Roy (ed.), cited in note 17, pp. 85–9 and p. 101.

29. Ibid., p. 85 and pp. 95–7.

30. E. Martin and A. Duval, 'Les deux variétés de jaune de plomb et d'étain: étude chronologique', *Studies in Conservation*, 35, 1990, pp. 117–25.

31. Kühn, cited in note 28, pp. 95–6.

32. Verdigris particle types are sometimes recognisable in paint cross-sections, particularly thin sections, by comparison with scanning electron micrographs of standard specimens. In the greens from the *Allegories*, blue basic verdigris ($[Cu(Ac)_2]_2.Cu(OH)_2.5H_2O$) and green basic verdigris ($Cu(Ac)_2.[Cu(OH)_2]_3.2H_2O$) were identified. See Kühn, 'Verdigris and Copper Resinate', A. Roy (ed.), cited in note 17, pp. 134–5, fig. 5.

33. The chloride is present at relatively low levels and seems not to indicate the use of an artificial basic copper chloride pigment such as atacamite or calumetite. More likely it is a residual component from one of the traditional methods for preparing verdigris, involving exposing to acetic acid vapour copper plates coated in common salt (sodium chloride) bound with honey. See, for example, recipe no.85, 'to make verdigris', in Mrs Merrifield's translation of the Bolognese MS, in *Original Treatises on the Arts of Painting*, Vol.II, 1849, p. 418.

34. Mills and White, cited in note 26.

35. Natural arsenic(II) sulphide can exist in several polymorphs. A new form, pararealgar, was identified in 1980 and the first occurrence in a painting was reported in 1995. See M.-C. Corbeil and K. Helwig, 'An occurrence of pararealgar as an original or altered artists' pig-

ment', *Studies in Conservation*, 40, 1995, pp. 133–8. These authors point out that the pararealgar could have resulted from the transformation of realgar.

36. T. Pignatti, *Veronese*, 2 vols., Venice 1976, I, no. 256, p. 150; R. Pallucchini, *Veronese*, Milan 1984, no. 232, p. 232 and p. 186; Rearick, cited in note 3, no. 71, p. 139.

37. Pignatti, cited in note 36, I, nos. 84–90, 120–2, pp. 116, 124; II, figs. 176–84, 362–4.

38. K. Brugnolo Meloncelli, *Battista Zelotti*, Milan 1992, cat.21, pp. 101–2; figs. 122–3.

39. Ibid. cat. 18, p. 100; figs. 91–4.

40. For the engraving by a follower of Marcantonio see Bartsch, *Le Peintre Graveur*, XIV, no. 460 (*The Illustrated Bartsch*), XXVII (ed. K. Oberhuber), New York 1978, no. 460 (342). Chiaroscuro prints after the Marcantonio were made by Zanetti in the eighteenth century. It is sometimes claimed (e.g. by Rearick, cited in note 3, p. 139) that Veronese's source was a chiaroscuro print and specifically one by Ugo da Carpi. There may be a confusion between Ugo da Carpi's print of a sibyl after Raphael and the Zanetti (see *The Illustrated Bartsch*, XLVIII (ed. C. Karpinski), New York 1983, pp. 138–9, 340–1). The drawing upon which Marcantonio's print is based is certainly among the most Parmigianesque of Raphael's drawings, and was generally regarded as by Parmigianino at the time of the first edition of Gould's catalogue, but no authority has doubted the attribution to Raphael since the brilliant article by Konrad Oberhuber, 'Eine unbekannte Zeichnung Raffaels in den Uffizien', *Mitteilungen des Kunsthistorischen Institutes in Florenz*, XII, 1966, pp. 225–44.

41. Gould, cited in note 1, p. 325.

42. Carlo Ridolfi, *Le Maraviglie dell'Arte*, 2 vols., ed. D. von Hadeln, Berlin 1914, I, p. 310, note 3.

43. For example Pignatti, cited in note 36, I, no. 206, p. 141, expressing agreement with Pallucchini and observing the 'sontuosità raffinatissima'. Rearick, cited in note 3, p. 139, dates the picture 'about 1558' but gives no reasons for doing so.

44. The painting measures 197.5 x 115.6 cm. The narrow strip (*c*. 15 cm not including the tacking edge) along the left edge is joined by a vertical seam. The larger piece is therefore almost exactly a metre in width but, with the tacking edge, would originally have measured a little more than a metre. The thread count, measured from the X-ray, is on average 10×10 threads per cm.

45. $CaSO_4.2H_2O$ identified by X-ray diffraction (in agreement with JCPDS file no. 6–46).

46. *Gesso sottile* is rehydrated calcium sulphate, prepared by slaking burnt gypsum. Raw gypsum

is also calcium sulphate dihydrate, and therefore indistinguishable from *gesso sottile* by X-ray diffraction but, given the coarse texture of raw gypsum, it seems more likely that the ground here is *gesso sottile*.

47. E. Martin, N. Sonoda, A.R. Duval, 'Contribution à l'étude des préparations blanches des tableaux italiens sur bois', *Studies in Conservation*, 37, 1992, pp. 82–92.

48. Smalt, a blue cobalt-containing glass, was identified by EDX.

49. Many of the particles show a loss of colour around their edges, only the core remaining blue. See Mühlethaler and Thissen, 'Smalt', in A. Roy (ed.), cited in note 17, pp. 116–21.

50. Vermilion, and the alumina substrate used in the preparation of the red lake pigment, were identified by EDX analysis on a cross-section.

51. EDX analysis indicated that the bright yellow pigment in paint from the orange drapery contained As. The appearance under the microscope was characteristic of orpiment (arsenic[III] sulphide), rather than the yellow polymorph of arsenic(II) sulphide pararealgar (see note 35).

52. For example, G.P. Lomazzo, *Trattato dell'arte de la pintura*, Milan 1584, Libro Terzo: Del Colore, Cap.VI, p. 193. 'L'oro pimento è nemico di tutti i colori, saluo che del giesso, ocrea, azurri, smalti, verdi azurri, terra verde, morel di ferro, endico, maiolica, e lacca'. (Orpiment is an enemy to all save gypsum, ochre, azures, smalt, green azure, green earth, rust of iron, brown of Spain and lake.)

53. Identified by X-ray diffraction, in agreement with JCPDS file no. 17–607.

54. See Kühn, cited in note 28, pp. 99–111. Results of analyses carried out by X-ray diffraction at the National Gallery are published in this article, together with Kühn's results; the reported occurrences of lead-tin yellow 'type II' in the sixteenth century are all in Venetian paintings.

55. Kühn, cited in note 28, p. 91. Kühn notes that although both types of lead-tin yellow are usually of small particle size, larger particles sometimes occur in samples of the 'type II' form.

56. First noted by F. Sansovino, *Venetia città noblissima et singolare*, Venice 1581, fol.65r. Neither this nor any subsequent Venetian guide describes it as an altarpiece. That it was on the left of the church is clear from the *Descrizione* of Boschini and Zanetti in 1733 (p. 269) and there is no reason to suppose that it had moved between then and 1821 when A. Quadri in *Otto Giorni a Venezia* (I, 1821, p. 273) describes it as hanging *between* the second and third altars. Interestingly, Eastlake himself never seems to have described it as an altarpiece. Moreover, it is considerably wider than any other painting by

Veronese or Tintoretto that is known to have hung above an altar.

57. *Annual Report of the National Gallery for 1856*, p. 27, and MS Minutes of the Board, IV (1855–71), pp. 6–8 (for Eastlake's letter of 12 November 1855 proposing the purchase) and pp. 17–19 (for his report of 9 February 1856).

58. Minutes of the Board, cited in note 57 above. In October 1855 the painting was packed up for transport to Paris where it was to be offered to Baron James Rothschild. Otto Mundler engineered its diversion, but, even after the sale of the painting, a higher offer was (according to Eastlake) made by a person who had 'before endeavoured to come to an arrangement' with the vendor (probably an allusion to the Baron).

59. Gould, cited in note 1, pp. 318–19.

60. Gould, cited in note 1, p. 319.

61. Richter's report of Morelli's opinion is given in a letter to A.M. Daniel of 8 January 1932 (National Gallery Archives). Waterhouse had a few years previously convinced himself that none of the painting was by Veronese (his note in the Gallery's dossier).

62. Pignatti, cited in note 36, I, no. 231, pp. 144–5; II, figs. 545 and 546.

63. Pen and brown ink heightened with white on pale (faded) blue paper, 27.8 x 20.2 cm. Teylers Museum, Haarlem, B65. For a full discussion of the drawing see Rearick, cited in note 3, no. 58, pp. 115–16. He, however, makes no mention of the altarpiece in S. Corona which, as Gould correctly notes, also owes something to ideas sketched out here.

64. The standard loom width for paintings in Venice, from measurements on paintings, appears to be just over one metre.

65. EDX analysis on cross-sections showed that there were some large particles containing Al, Si and K.

66. R.J. Gettens, E. West Fitzhugh and R.L. Feller, 'Calcium Carbonate Whites', in A. Roy (ed.), cited in note 17, pp. 203–26. A mixture of calcite and gypsum in the ground on a polychrome statue by Donatello is reported in this article. Two tentative explanations are put forward: the gypsum may have been overheated forming CaO which eventually converts to calcium carbonate; alternatively, the calcite may be an impurity in the mineral gypsum.

67. Calcite identified by X-ray diffraction, in agreement with JCPDS file no. 5–586.

68. Rearick, cited in note 3, p. 102. A fresco of the Venetian Triumph in the Guise of Neptune by Veronese for the façade of the Palazzo Erizzo (now lost) is documented by a drawing now in the Louvre.

69. Gettens, West Fitzhugh and Feller, cited in note 66. It is unlikely that raw limestone was used;

the calcium carbonate may have been in the form of lime plaster (slaked quicklime), which over a period of time forms calcium carbonate by reaction with carbon dioxide in the air. See Gettens et al. for a description of the preparation of lime for *buon fresco*.

71. Drawings for the figures are reproduced in Rearick, cited in note 3.

72. Malachite identified by X-ray diffraction, in agreement with JCPDS file no. 10–399.

73. Penny and Spring, cited in note 17.

74. Plesters, Roy and Bomford, cited in note 14.

75. Lead-tin yellow 'type II' identified by X-ray diffraction, in agreement with JCPDS file no. 17–607.

76. See Corbeil and Helwig, cited in note 35. Pararealgar was identified by X-ray diffraction, in agreement with the data in this article (JCPDS file no. 33–127).

77. HPLC analysis by Jo Kirby, see p. 71 in this *Bulletin*.

78. See Jo Kirby, 'The Identification of Red Lake Pigment Dyestuffs', p. 63 and p. 71 in this *Bulletin*.

79. L. Lazzarini, 'I materiali e la tecnica del *Convito in casa di Levi* di Paolo Veronese', *Quaderni della Soprintendenza ai beni artistici e storici di Venezia, Il Restauro del Convito in casa di Levi di Paolo Veronese*, Venice 1984, pp. 65–72.

80. Pignatti, cited in note 36, I, no. A.62, p. 117; II, fig. 777. Pignatti is not unusual in questioning the autograph status of this work.

81. Ibid., I, no. 343, p. 168; Rearick, cited in note 3, no. 103, pp. 198–200.

82. Inv. 447. See the entry by G.B. Molli in *Da Bellini a Tintoretto. Dipinti dei Musei civici di Padova*, ed. A. Ballarin and D. Banzato, Padua 1991, no. 118, pp. 198–9.

83. The earliest surviving paintings on slate are portraits by Sebastiano del Piombo of Clement VII (J. Paul Getty Museum, Malibu) and of Baccio Valori (Palazzo Pitti, Florence), and a battle painting (private collection, unpublished) by Girolamo da Treviso. For a general survey of paintings on stone see the introductory essay by Marco Chiarini in the catalogue of the exhibition *Pittura su Pietra* at Palazzo Pitti, May – June 1970. In Venice, Titian painted an *Addolorata* on slate (Prado, Madrid), sending this to Charles V in 1554, doubtless in emulation of Sebastiano's work, which was known to the Spanish Court. The large altarpiece by Federico Zuccaro dated 1564 in the Grimani Chapel of S. Francesco della Vigna is painted on stone (said to be marble) and later altarpieces executed in Rome by Federico Zuccaro and others are on sheets of slate joined

horizontally. Slate was also established as a popular support in Florence by the 1560s. Sebastiano is clearly stated by Vasari to have used coloured marbles and porphyry as well as slate supports, and these may well have been left partly exposed. Such was certainly the case in many small paintings of the late sixteenth century. One of the earliest among these is an oval *Adoration of the Magi*, painted on lapis lazuli which is left bare for the blue sky, which has been convincingly attributed to Jacopo Bassano and dated to the 1560s by G.M. Pilo (*Arte Veneta*, XXIX, 1975, pp. 167–73); and there is also a pair of octagonal *Adorations* (one of the Kings, the other of the Shepherds) by Jacopo Bassano, of similar date (with Piero Corsini in New York in 1986), painted on an orange pink *breccia* (stated in the dealers' catalogue to be Verona marble) where this serves as the sunset sky. A painting on black stone by Jacopo Bassano is mentioned in an inventory, and that he painted on this support is referred to by early biographers. Given the example of these paintings on lapis lazuli and *breccia* it would seem likely that he experimented with leaving the black stone to stand for the night sky. However, we know of no surviving painting earlier than Veronese's *Crucifixion* in which this device is found – it became, of course, a standard feature in works by later Veronese artists in this mode – Alessandro Turchi, Felice Brusasorchi, Pasquale Ottino, Marcantonio Bassetti, Giambattista Rovedato – whose work is well represented in the Castelvecchio Museum, Verona, as well as in the paintings by Bramer, Stella and others made elsewhere in Italy.

84. Pignatti, cited in note 36, I, no. 341, p. 167; II, figs. 715–16; Pallucchini, cited in note 36, no. 230, pp. 152, 186; Rearick, cited in note 3, no. 91, pp. 178–9.

85. Rearick, cited in note 3, no. 74, pp. 143–4 for a just estimate of this marvellous painting, much underestimated by earlier scholars. A dark grey layer can be clearly seen in the cracks (e.g. in the white dress and flesh of the Princess). The great *Calvary* of the Louvre is also painted on a grey preparation but one which is probably less dark.

86. H. Brigstocke, *Italian and Spanish Paintings in the National Gallery of Scotland*, 2nd ed., Edinburgh 1993, pp. 196–7, no. 339, and fig. 62 (X-radiograph).

87. *The Pietà with Two Saints and Saint Diego in Prayer* 'su rame, rovinatissimo' is in the Testa Chapel (last on the left side) of S. Giobbe. Lorenzetti, *Venezia e il suo estuario*, 1963 (Trieste reprint, 1982), p. 448.

The Identification of Red Lake Pigment Dyestuffs and a Discussion of their Use

JO KIRBY AND RAYMOND WHITE

On 23 February 1815, a lecture was read at the Royal Society giving an account of the experiments performed by Sir Humphrey Davy on early Roman pigments from wall paintings and sites in Rome then being excavated. One pigment, in a broken vase found at the baths of Titus, was 'a pale rose colour; where it has been exposed to air, it has lost its tint, ... but the interior has a lustre approaching to that of carmine.'[1] The effects of mineral acids and alkalis on the pigment and its behaviour on combustion suggested that it might be a lake, although, as it did not compare very well with modern samples of cochineal and madder lakes, Davy wondered if it might be Tyrian purple. In a note he commented that the French chemist Jean Chaptal had decided that the pale rose-coloured lake from Pompeii that he had examined contained a dyestuff of vegetable origin, because of 'its not affording by decomposition the smell peculiar to animal substances'.[2]

Our knowledge of the chemistry of organic substances has grown immeasurably since the early nineteenth century and methods for the analysis of naturally occurring dyestuffs have acquired a level of sophistication unimaginable to Davy and Chaptal. Progress in analysis has been achieved largely in the field of textile dyes, however; precise identification of what may well be the same colorants in traditional lake pigments has proved a more intractable problem. It has been necessary to rely on the evidence of pigment recipes and other documentary sources for much of the information at present available.

If a survey is made of the recipes used for the preparation of lake pigments between about 1400 and 1890, the dyestuffs most frequently mentioned are those extracted from brazilwood, madder, and the scale insects, kermes, cochineal and lac.[3] On the aluminium-containing substrates widely used up to the nineteenth century at least, madder gives a more orange red than the others, while lac and cochineal can give quite blue-toned crimsons (Plate 1).[4] The recipes indicate that the overall pattern of dyestuff usage changes over time. Up to the early seventeenth century, the sources of dyestuff appear to be brazilwood, lac and shearings of cloth dyed with kermes (and perhaps the different species of cochineal): the 'cimatura de grana' of fourteenth- and fifteenth-century Italian treatises.[5] The fact that madder is barely mentioned partly reflects the possibility that cloth shearings were also the source of this dyestuff; it may also reflect an accident of survival of the earlier written sources, or simply that those in the Flemish, Dutch or German dialects have so far been less thoroughly researched. It seems certain that there are strong links with the textile dyeing industry at this time. From the late sixteenth century onwards, the references to cochineal (the Central American species) become ever more frequent and the use of shearings appears to decrease. By the nineteenth century, the most important sources for artists' pigments appear to be cochineal and madder, lac and kermes being barely mentioned. The lack of durability of brazilwood dyestuff had long been known; it was not generally recommended for use as a high-quality artists' colour, although it was perfectly adequate for use in manuscripts, where it would receive relatively little light. The frequent mentions of brazilwood in earlier sources reflect the fact that many of these were written primarily for scribes and manuscript illuminators.

There are two principal difficulties in analysing a lake pigment dyestuff, the first of

56

Plate 1 Examples of dyed textiles and lake pigments. Foreground, left to right: kermes-dyed wool, kermes lake, brazilwood-dyed wool, brazilwood lake, madder-dyed wool, madder lake. Second row: lac lake, lac-dyed wool, cochineal-dyed wool (heavily dyed), cochineal lake. Painted glass plate (left to right): kermes, lac, cochineal and small sample of Polish cochineal, brazilwood and madder, all in linseed oil. At rear, silks dyed with kermes (dyed twice), cochineal (dyed once) and kermes (dyed once).

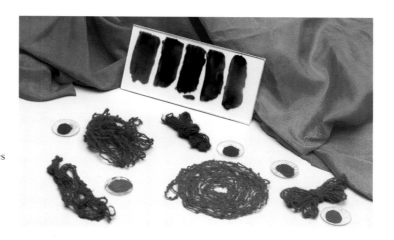

which is the small size of sample available. In a traditional lake pigment, the dyestuff is often present in quite low concentration. In a sample of the modern pigment alizarin crimson prepared in the laboratory, using a typical recipe, the amount of alizarin dyestuff used was approximately 30 per cent by weight of the final yield of pigment.[6] It is no surprise that the colour of alizarin crimson is very intense (Plate 2a). In contrast, the photomicrograph of a cross-section prepared from a sample of reddish-purplish paint from the robe of Saint Paul in *The Virgin and Child with Saints Peter and Paul* (NG 774), by Dieric Bouts, shows that a fifteenth-century madder lake is very much less intense in colour: the proportion of dyestuff in the lake, seen here mixed with the blue mineral pigment ultramarine, is very much lower (Plates 2b, 3). Admittedly not all early lakes contain a low concentration of dyestuff: some are extraordinarily intense in colour when examined under the microscope. A paint sample may consist of several layers of pigment bound in paint medium; only one of these may contain lake pigment. As traditional lake pigments are translucent they are frequently used as glazing pigments; applied over other paint even a thin glaze is very effective, indeed, as far as dyestuff content is concerned, perhaps deceptively so. The proportion of medium present in the glaze is usually quite high. This may be partly explained by a desire for transparency; also, in the case of lakes in an oil medium, a large proportion of oil is necessary to produce a workable paint, in other words, lake pigments have a high oil absorption. Thus even if the sample taken contains a high proportion of the glaze layer, very little lake pigment may be present.

The other principal impediment to dye identification has been the need to extract the colorant from the pigment for most analytical methods; in the case of a paint sample the pigment is bound up in the medium, rendering extraction difficult.

Methods of analysis

The methods generally used for the examination of dyestuffs can be divided into those based on electronic or vibrational spectrometry and those depending on chromatographic separation of the colorants into their individual components. The two may be combined, as in gas chromatography–mass spectrometry (GC–MS), for example, although the use of this particular technique for dyestuff analysis is not yet well developed. Chromatographic methods are the more precise and informative; certain spectrometric methods have the advantage that they may be used non-destructively on the object itself.

UV-visible absorption spectrophotometry, often used for dyestuffs in solution, can be used for pigment identification, but, using conventional equipment, is not an appropriate method for small samples from paintings.[7] Fluorescence spectrometry, which has been applied to the identification of naturally occurring dyestuffs in solutions of concentration 10^{-2} to $10^{-4} \mu g/ml$,[8] has, however, been applied successfully to the examination of dyestuffs extracted from paint samples.[9] Spectrophotometric methods where reflectance or transmittance spectra of the dyed textile, pigment or paint are measured directly

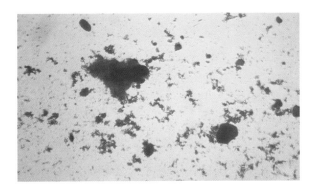

Plate 2a Roberson's alizarin crimson dispersed in immersion oil A. Original magnification 137.5 ×; actual magnification 110 ×.

Plate 2b Dieric Bouts, *The Virgin and Child with Saints Peter and Paul* (NG 774). Cross-section prepared from a sample of reddish-purple paint from the robe of Saint Paul, showing a glaze of madder lake and ultramarine over a layer comprising madder lake, azurite and lead white. There appears to be a pale grey priming (lead white mixed with carbon black) below this. The lowest layer is the chalk ground. Original magnification 750 ×; actual magnification 590 ×.

Plates 2a and b photographed under the microscope by reflected light.

are less sensitive, although, compared with earlier instruments, microspectrophotometers now available give greatly improved reflectance curves over a broader spectrum.[10] The method developed in the National Gallery Scientific Department for the measurement of spectral transmittance curves of lake pigments in particles or thin cross-sections of paint is capable of greater sensitivity.[11] Reflectance microspectrophotometry can be used for non-destructive examination of materials, but the red colorants most frequently encountered up to the late nineteenth century are not reliably identified by this method: in an examination of dyed textiles, for example, accurate distinction between kermes and cochineal dyestuffs was not possible.[12]

There is also the risk that mixtures of dyestuffs may be misinterpreted. Three-dimensional fluorescence spectrometry has been used as a non-destructive method of analysis on textile samples, but the instrumentation described is not suitable for paintings.[13]

Methods of analysis based on vibrational spectrometry have been less successful; although useful results have been obtained from naturally occurring colorants with an indigoid molecular structure, natural red dyestuffs do not come into this category. In practice the size of paint sample available for analysis has usually been too small for conventional infra-red spectrometry to be used. Fourier transform infra-red (FTIR) spectrometry, in which resolution is enhanced, is more powerful; when linked to an infra-red microscope the examination of small samples becomes possible. Since the use of FTIR was first proposed it has been applied to textile dyestuff analysis; it is rendered more complicated if the presence of bands from the mordant and the fibre must also be taken into account, as well as, perhaps, the effects of changes in the materials with time.[14] If a preliminary separation of the dyestuff components is carried out using thin-layer chromatography (TLC), FTIR may then be used for their identification.[15] Although spectra may be obtained from samples of lake pigment prepared in the laboratory, little success has been achieved with samples from paintings.[16] Raman resonance spectroscopy, coupled with a microscope, has been used with some success as a non-destructive method for the identification of inorganic pigments in manuscripts.[17] The identification of many natural organic dyestuffs is more difficult as the Raman signal is easily swamped by fluorescence from the dyestuffs themselves and from other organic materials present. While this can to some extent be filtered out by changing the excitation wavelength of the incident radiation, very few analyses of lake pigments or textiles containing natural dyestuffs have been reported.[18]

Thin-layer chromatography (TLC) has been used for extensive studies of red textile dyestuffs and, more recently, research on the constituents of naturally occurring and early synthetic textile colorants.[19] The method has also been applied to the analysis of lake pigments.[20] For several years a method derived from that developed using cellulose acetate plates was used at the National Gallery for the analysis of lake pigment dyestuffs; the substrate used was 85 per cent Polyamide 11, 15 per cent cellulose acetate (Macherey Nagel MN300 Ac-10), the plates being coated in the laboratory. This was found to give better separation and definition for hydroxyanthraquinone dyestuffs extracted from paint samples than cellulose acetate alone. The eluent used was chloroform/methanol/ethyl methyl ketone/acetyl acetone in the proportions 8:10:5:1. In the late 1970s it became impossible to obtain the cellulose acetate powder and the method was discontinued in favour of high performance liquid chromatography.

In the last few years, high performance liquid chromatography (HPLC) has permitted quantitative identification of the constituents of colorants extracted from textiles and also from the source materials.[21] Such detailed study can assist in the taxonomic separation of closely related scale insect species; it has also enabled a more accurate distinction between, for example, the dyestuffs extracted from the Old and New World cochineal insects, the principal constituent of which is carminic acid in each case.[22] The research has been aided considerably by the use of a computerised diode-array detector, which permits detection at a wavelength range of 200–800nm and also allows the acquisition of a UV-visible absorption spectrum of a component during or after the analysis.[23] If the sample cell is to have an adequate window area for sufficient transmitted energy to fall on the detector, however, it must have a minimum internal volume of about 10μl. The amount of lake pigment dyestuff which can be extracted from a paint sample is usually so small that dilution to this cell volume weakens absorption to too great an extent; this has therefore limited the number of occasions when this method of detection of lake pigment dyestuffs has been possible.[24]

Experimental details

In order to use high performance liquid chromatography to examine lake pigment dyestuffs in paint samples, it has been necessary to accept certain limitations imposed by the small sample size and low dyestuff concentration. The use of microbore columns gives potentially higher

Plate 3 Dieric Bouts, *The Virgin and Child with Saints Peter and Paul* (NG 774), probably 1460s. Oak, 68.6 × 51.4 cm.

chromatographic resolution and a considerable reduction in solvent volume, minimising dilution of separated components. The apparatus can easily be interfaced with the mass spectrometer, enabling further characterisation of the separated components. A disadvantage is that run times are very long. The choice of detector has been limited by the system chosen, which necessitates the use of a small detector cell volume, about 0.8μl, for good resolution at low flow rates of 10–20μl (one-hundredth of that for the conventional system). Until recently, the absorption cells in commercial diode-array detectors were too large to be used with a microbore system, although new developments in technology will help solve this problem. The disadvantage of the present system is that the detector and amplification system used appear to have about one-tenth of the sensitivity of more recent detectors, using carminic acid as a standard.[25]

Analysis is carried out on a modified system

derived from Shimadzu LC-5A microbore HPLC modular components, adapted in this laboratory to provide gradient elution facilities. The apparatus consists of two LC-5A pumps under the control of a GRE-3A gradient controller, each connected by way of an SSI LP-21 damping unit to a Lee Visco Mixer (3μl hold-up volume). The eluent mixture is fed directly to a Rheodyne type 8125 injector fitted with a 2.5μl sample loop. Chromatographic separation is carried out using three 50cm Shimadzu ODS-18 reversed phase microbore columns connected in series. The effluent from the column is fed to a SPD-2AM variable wavelength UV spectrophotometric detector (range c.195–350nm), fitted with a 0.8μl internal volume flow cell, by way of an adjustable-split T-junction. The split ratio is set to about 4 to 1 in favour of the UV detector, the other line being connected to a VG Biotech Trio 2000 mass spectrometer, coupled by means of an electrospray/ionspray interface. The outlet from the flow cell is fitted with a SSI adjustable back pressure valve, set to about 3 atmospheres pressure (c.280kPa), to prevent bubble formation in the detector cell.

The solvent system has two components, (A) 94.9% water/0.1% trifluoroacetic acid/5% acetonitrile and (B) 95% methanol/5% acetonitrile, purged with helium before and during use. The presence of an acid in the eluent system was found necessary to suppress hydrogen ion formation, causing multiple, and tailing, chromatographic peaks. Originally acetic and formic acids were tried; these were replaced by o-phosphoric acid (2%) because of drifting retention times and poor peak shape, which deteriorated during the course of the run and was probably due to formation of esters with the methanol.[26] When examination of the colorants by electrospray-mass spectrometry commenced, it became apparent that molecular and fragment ionisation were suppressed and o-phosphoric acid was replaced by trifluoroacetic acid: at a concentration below 0.5%, minimal ion suppression is observed while chromatographic peak shape remains acceptable. The eluents are held at the starting concentration of 70%A : 30%B for 15 minutes; the concentration of B is then increased by 1%/minute to 45%, then by 0.5%/minute to the final concentration of 25%A : 75%B. The run is allowed to continue at this concentration for as long as

necessary at a flow rate of 20μl/minute, the total run time being about six hours. The detection wavelength used for red dyestuffs is 275nm: not necessarily the optimum detection wavelength for every dyestuff component, but the most useful on average. It permits the detection of yellow dyestuff components which may also be present, although for these a detection wavelength of 255nm gives better results. The amplifier time constant is set to 2.5 seconds. Readings are at present logged on a Grant Squirrel recorder, type 1202, sampling at one reading a second; the range scale is set at 200mV (1mV being equivalent to 1×10^{-3}AU).

For the analysis of textile dyestuffs, the colorant is normally dissolved out using dilute hydrochloric or sulphuric acids mixed with an organic solvent such as methanol or ethyl acetate, followed by extraction into a suitable solvent.[27] Acid hydrolysis is not a satisfactory method for breaking up a highly polymerised paint film: transmethylation is more effective. The methylating agent boron trifluoride-methanol not only breaks up the paint medium,[28] but also, conveniently, dissolves the dyestuff out of the lake pigment. It has been found, however, that certain dyestuff constituents are altered to the extent that the colorant is no longer recognisable if the reagent is used at full strength and heated as in the standard procedure for methylation, kermes being particularly vulnerable; the commercially available reagent is therefore diluted to approximately 5 per cent. At this concentration partial methylation of the dyestuff components usually occurs, the degree depending on the quantity and strength of the reagent and for how long it remains in contact with the sample before analysis, as well as on the chemical structure of the components. It is advisable to test the strength of the reagent on a known pigment sample before use. 5μl ≈ 5% boron trifluoride-methanol are added to the sample which is then agitated in the ultrasonic bath and allowed to stand overnight; usually no further treatment is carried out, other than to centrifuge the sample before withdrawing a 2.5μl aliquot for injection onto the column.

The presence of the paint medium in the sample solution rarely causes more than minor inconvenience, unless it is very discoloured or present in great excess. It is possible to extract the medium from the paint, before examination of the dyestuff, using *m*-(trifluoromethyl) phenyltrimethylammonium hydroxide (TMTFTH).[29] The effect of the reagent on the dyestuffs is variable, but if the sample is left in contact with the reagent for as short a time as possible the dyestuff should be unaffected. Laboratory trials suggest that use of the reagent should be avoided with yellow lake pigments and if the paint is relatively recent (mid-nineteenth century or later). The residue from the treatment is washed very thoroughly with methanol to remove all traces of the reagent before addition of boron trifluoride-methanol, otherwise residual reagent produces a strong chromatographic peak in approximately the same region as alizarin. There is, of course, no reason why the residue should not be treated by acid hydrolysis as conventionally done; this will result in hydrolysis of the O–glycosides and probably certain other components eluted in this region of the chromatogram.

Results

The system was developed on a pragmatic basis to enable analysis of an important class of pigments about which frustratingly little was known, hindering study of the Gallery collection from a historical point of view, and from that of conservation. The intention has been to rectify this; primary research on the dyestuffs themselves has already been very well covered. The method used gives satisfactory and reproducible results under the conditions stated; background research into mechanistic aspects is necessarily of secondary importance and therefore proceeding at a slower pace.

Preliminary indications are that, under the conditions employed, partial methylation of carboxylic and possibly some activated phenolic functions takes place. This is illustrated in Figs. 1a and 1b. Fig. 1a shows the chromatogram of an aqueous extract of lac dyestuff from stick lac, the reddish or yellowish resin-like material secreted by *Kerria lacca* Kerr and other species, which forms an encrustation on the twigs of trees upon which the insects live, enveloping the insects themselves.[30] The dyestuff contains a mixture of laccaic acids, the principal constituents being laccaic acids A and B.[31] Fig. 1b shows the chromatogram of a sample of lac lake prepared in the laboratory, after treat-

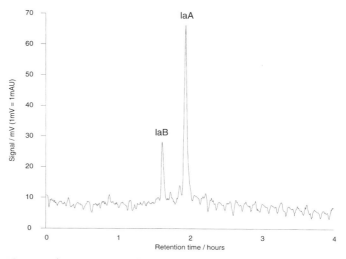

Fig. 1a Chromatogram of aqueous extract of lac dyestuff from stick lac (*Kerria* sp.); laA: laccaic acid A; laB: laccaic acid B. Eluents and conditions described in the text.

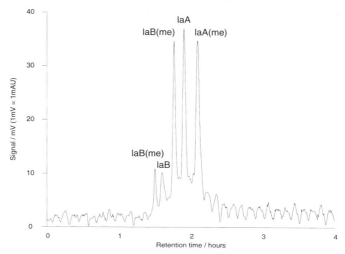

Fig. 1b Chromatogram of lac lake (prepared in the laboratory), after treatment with 5% boron trifluoride- methanol; laA, laB: laccaic acids A and B; laA(me), laB(me): methylated derivatives of laccaic acids A and B.

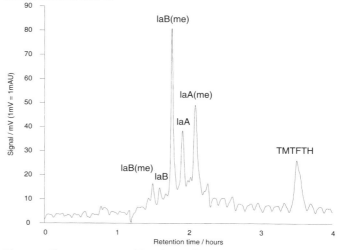

Fig. 1c Chromatogram of lac dyestuff extracted from sample of the red cloak, from *Cardinal Richelieu* (NG 1449), painted by Philippe de Champaigne, *c*.1637; after extraction of paint medium with TMTFTH, a trace of which has produced the peak thus labelled. Laccaic acids as before.

Plate 4 Philippe de Champaigne, *Cardinal Richelieu* (NG 1449), *c*.1637. Canvas, 259.7 × 177.8 cm.

ment with 5% boron trifluoride-methanol as described; the laccaic acid B complex tends to be methylated to a very much greater extent than laccaic acid A.

If the period of methylation is extended or the treatment is performed at a higher temperature, the proportion of derivatised components increases. If the reaction is pushed towards completion, which would be the normal practice, successful identification of the colorant is rendered more difficult. Fully derivatised laccaic and carminic acids are poorly resolved under these chromatographic conditions: unfortunately some compromise has had to be made with the eluent and gradient systems at present available and a ternary or quaternary gradient programming regime would undoubtedly be the ideal solution. Fully derivatised kermes dyestuff components are degraded; in earlier years, when more complete derivatisation was used with TLC as described above, occasional misidentification of kermes-containing lake pigments is known to have occurred. An example is the deep purple cloth of honour in Gerard David's *The Virgin and Child with Saints and a Donor* (NG 1432),

painted in about 1510, which is painted in a red lake pigment mixed with azurite. Two analyses by TLC in 1978 indicated the presence of cochineal lake, apparently from the New World insect *Dactylopius coccus* Costa, a surprising result as it is unlikely that samples of the insects reached Spain before the 1520s or 30s and the earliest documented date for the import of the dyestuff into Europe is in the 1540s.[32] When another sample from the same robe was re-examined using HPLC (see Table 2, p. 72), carminic acid (the colouring matter of cochineal) was found to be present, but the principal dyestuff was that extracted from kermes, not identified previously because of degradation by the reagent. It is more likely that the lake pigment contains the dyestuff from an Old World insect, perhaps Polish cochineal, *Porphyrophora polonica* L., which contains a proportion of kermesic acid, mixed with kermes dyestuff.

Fig. 1c shows the chromatogram of lac dyestuff extracted from a sample of the dark red glaze of Cardinal Richelieu's cloak in Philippe de Champaigne's *Cardinal Richelieu* (NG 1449), painted in about 1637 (Plate 4). The principal laccaic acids and their methylated derivatives are clearly discernible. The sample had previously been treated with TMTFTH to extract the paint medium; the broad peak with a retention time of about 210 minutes is due to residual traces of this reagent.

While retention times generally remain consistent to about ±1–2%, they can be affected by changes in the ambient conditions, particularly temperature. It is therefore necessary to run standard samples for comparison (known pigments prepared in the laboratory, for example) or, preferably, to use an internal standard, measuring retention times relative to this.[33] To date, no entirely satisfactory internal standard for the system used has been found.

The principal component of the dyestuff extracted from brazilwood (*Caesalpinia* spp.) is the 4-arylchroman, brazilin, which forms brazilein on oxidation.[34] The main constituent of the freshly-extracted colorant is eluted at *c*. 88 minutes; treatment with the reagent causes degradation, giving a typical pattern of peaks at about 88, 97, 107 and 119 minutes. For comparison, the yellow flavonoid dye luteolin, found in weld and dyers' broom, is eluted at about 141 minutes.

The results obtained from paint samples are given in Table 2 (pp. 70–3). In several cases it has been possible to confirm and occasionally to amplify results obtained earlier by TLC. There is, however, a limit to what can be deduced from these chromatograms. Comparison of chromatograms given by paint samples containing a cochineal dyestuff and those given by standard solutions of carminic acid suggests that the amount of dyestuff present in the paint samples is usually about 1–2µg: 1 or 2 per cent of the weight of a paint sample about 0.5mm² in size, containing other pigments and medium as well as the lake. Taking into account contributions from the paint medium (and perhaps from materials used in conservation treatments) to the chromatogram obtained and the limit of detection of the system in use, it is unrealistic to make any quantitative measures of individual dyestuff constituents or of their relative proportions when minor components must frequently fail to be detected. The published detailed studies of the dyestuff constituents have been based on extracts from the raw materials and dyed textiles; it has yet to be established how far the results of this research can be applied to the results obtained from lake pigment dyestuffs, particularly if these were extracted from textile waste: they may or may not be comparable. It should also be remembered that the amount of dyestuff available in the raw material and the proportions of its constituents will vary according to the time of year at which the material was harvested, the climatic and environmental conditions, and, in the case of lac for example, the host plant.[37] This is quite apart from the fact that the dyestuff constitution of plants often varies according to the part of the plant used and at different stages in the development of both scale insect and plant sources.[38]

In practice, this has had a bearing on the distinction between Old and New World cochineal insects, as well as on the further investigation of mixtures of dyestuffs such as kermes and madder, or kermes and cochineal. The principal dyestuff in cochineal insects is carminic acid. Polish cochineal, *Porphyrophora polonica* L. (Fig. 2),[39] which once occurred widely across Europe in Poland and other regions with light, sandy soils, also contains a

Table 1

Typical retention times (in minutes) for some of the principal dyestuff constituents[35]

laccaic acid B	97
methylated laccaic acid B	91, 106
carminic acid	107
laccaic acid A	117
methylated laccaic acid A	126
methylated carminic acid	125
flavokermesic acid (laccaic acid D)	161
kermesic acid	172
alizarin	214
methylated flavokermesic acid	232
methylated kermesic acid	258
purpurin[36]	*c*.350

variable proportion of flavokermesic and kermesic acids (the colouring matter found in kermes), equivalent to perhaps 6–9 per cent or more, depending on the method of processing.[40] Armenian or Ararat cochineal, *Porphyrophora hamelii* Brandt, which occurs principally in saline marshes in Armenia and Azerbaijan, contains very much less of these acids and without investigation of other minor components is hard to distinguish from the Central American insect *Dactylopius coccus* Costa.[41] If Polish cochineal dyestuff is present in low concentration (or if other organic constituents of the paint sample interfere) the small proportion of kermesic and flavokermesic acids may not be detected. Similarly, at these very low dyestuff concentrations, a mixture containing mainly the New World cochineal insect dyestuff with a small proportion extracted from kermes, *Kermes vermilio* Planchon, could be incorrectly identified. As a result it has not always been possible to state which cochineal insect was used; indeed, during the later sixteenth and early seventeenth centuries, when the Polish and New World insects were both available and in use in Western Europe, it would be perfectly possible to find a mixture of the two. By this time, however, the ready availability of the New World insect and frequent documentary references to it suggest that it was a more likely source of dye than the Armenian insect, in Western Europe at least.

Discussion of results

Circumstances have dictated that a large proportion of the paintings examined date from the period between 1400 and 1600 and, within this group, rather more than half are assigned to Italian schools. In spite of this, a number of general points can be made.

If one considers the fifteenth and early part of the sixteenth centuries, and if it is also assumed that the paintings examined were fairly standard commissions, it can be seen that, broadly speaking, painters working in Italian city states and regions (Florence, Siena, Venice, Ferrara and other parts of Northern Italy) tended to use lake pigments prepared from scale insect dyestuffs, whereas those working in Northern Europe tended to use those prepared from madder, later with the addition of kermes. Relatively few results have so far been obtained from Northern European paintings and the pattern they form is less clear. Much later, during the seventeenth century, the use of the New World cochineal insect becomes widespread. This bears out the evidence suggested by the recipes. Brazilwood-containing lakes appear to have been little used; it is clear that brazilwood was not thought to be as good quality as other dyestuffs and probably its absence is partly explained by this.[42] It has also been suggested, on the basis of results from the analysis of textile dyestuffs, that brazilwood may have been unavailable in Europe from about the time of the fall of Constantinople in 1453 – which may have disrupted the supply of sappan wood, *Caesalpinia sappan* L., from the East – until the discovery of the New World species *C. brasiliensis* L. (brazilwood), *C. crista* L. (fernambuco wood) and *C. echinata* Lam (peachwood).[43] The poor permanence of the colour from these woods, which were imported into Europe soon after 1500, soon became apparent. In 1553, William Cholmeley described brazilwood as 'disceytfull' and 'a fauls colour' and his was a common complaint;[44] it would be interesting to know if they were any more or less 'disceytfull' than sappan wood in this respect.

Very much more is known about the use of the same dyestuffs on textiles over the same period. In Italy, kermes, Polish cochineal and, later, New World cochineal were used to a greater extent for high quality textile dyeing

Fig. 2 Stages in the life cycle of Polish cochineal, here seen as cysts on the roots of the perennial knawel; the adult insect, drawings 11–15, is compared with the adult Mexican cochineal insect, drawings A–C. From J.P. Breynius, *Historia naturalis cocci tinctorii, quod polonicum vulgo audit*, 1731.[39]
By permission of The British Library.

Plate 5 Altobello Melone, *Christ carrying the Cross* (NG 6546), *c*.1520–5. Poplar, 49 × 63.5 cm.

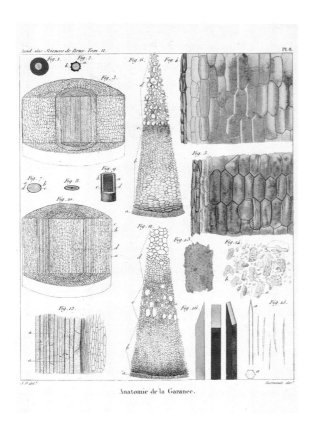

Anatomie de la Garance.

Plate 6 Structure of the madder root, in transverse and longitudinal section, at different stages in its development. Diagrams 4 and 5 illustrate the change in colour of the cut surface of the root from yellow to red on exposure to the air. Diagram 16 shows crystals of alizarin; for their colour, Decaisne used those obtained by Robiquet who, with Colin, was responsible for the isolation of alizarin and purpurin from madder in 1826. From J. Decaisne, 'Recherches anatomiques et physiologiques sur la garance', 1837.[50] By permission of The British Library.

than brazilwood or madder; lac was rarely used. In Northern Europe – Flanders, the Netherlands and Germany – madder was the most important dyestuff in the fifteenth and sixteenth centuries, kermes and the other scale insects being apparently little used before the sixteenth century. The use of New World cochineal grew in importance during the later sixteenth and seventeenth centuries.[45] However, guild statutes and records of duties payable for the movement of goods indicate that madder was available in Italy by the thirteenth century, but, like brazilwood, it was probably considered appropriate for different uses, then and later.[46] A closer study of both the results of analysis and dyeing recipes indicates that before the mid-sixteenth century, for example, madder was used to dye wool and silk in Venice and other Italian

cities (but not what one would imagine to be the most expensive fabrics) while, shortly afterwards, cochineal was similarly used in Antwerp.[47] A greater range of goods, including dyestuffs, would be available around major international trading centres like Antwerp and Venice.[48] Perhaps on this account it is interesting that the single sixteenth-century example of madder lake identified so far in an Italian painting occurs in a work by a North Italian artist: *Christ carrying the Cross* (NG 6546), painted in the early 1520s by the Cremonese painter Altobello Melone (Plate 5; Table 2, p. 71). Similarly, kermes has been identified on sixteenth-century tapestries from Antwerp and Brussels, while kermes-containing lakes have been found in paintings by Gerard David, who worked in Bruges and Antwerp around 1484–1523, Ambrosius Benson, who worked in Bruges around 1518–50 (Table 2, p. 72), and in a group of altarpieces painted in Antwerp between 1495–1560.[49]

Over a long period the Netherlands, notably Zeeland and especially the region around Schouwen, were celebrated for the quality of the madder produced, while Southern France, Spain and other areas around the Mediterranean were the source of kermes. In madder, *Rubia tinctorum* L., and related species, the dyestuff constituents are found predominantly in the root, largely in the form of glycosides. The principal anthraquinones, alizarin and pseudopurpurin, occur largely as primverosides, the yellow colour of which can be seen if the root is broken; the colour of the broken surface gradually changes to red as the anthraquinones (which taste unpleasant and presumably have a protective function for the plant) are released (Plate 6).[50] The dyestuff is found under the bark of the root and through the central part; this portion, without the bark and outer matter, was the best, the so-called *krap* madder, and was the final product of pounding in the madder mill. The first product, *mull*, containing the most dirt, outer materials and tiny roots, was the worst (in eighteenth-century France it was known as *billon* and discarded); there were also other grades.[51] The grades, and the amount of dirt each was permitted to contain, were already fixed in the fifteenth century, as the Reymerswaal regulations for the production of madder of 1480 make clear.[52] The number of references to madder and its production in official documents in the Netherlands from the fourteenth century onwards indicate that the dyestuff was the centre of a highly developed industry.[53]

Although there are several species of *Kermes*, only one, *Kermes vermilio* Planchon, which occurs on the kermes oak *Quercus coccifera* L. (Fig. 3),[54] is of importance for its dyestuff. Another insect, *K. ballotae* Signoret, an albino form of *K. vermilio* Planchon, may occur on the same host tree. The dyestuff extracted from this insect contains about 80 per cent of yellowish flavokermesic acid, with only about 20 per cent of kermesic acid, the principal constituent of the *K. vermilio* dyestuff; the presence of significant quantities of this insect in the dyebath would thus adversely affect the final colour.[55] Italian sources of the fourteenth to sixteenth centuries refer to kermes (and apparently Old World cochineals, depending on the date of the source) under the name of *grana*. The Florentine merchant Francesco Balducci Pegolotti, in his merchants' handbook written around 1339–40, lists seven different types, including *grana di Schiavonia*, while the late fourteenth- or early fifteenth-century manual of the Florentine Arte della Seta, mentions *grana di cintri*, *Spagnuola*, *le barbaresche*, *la Valenza* and *la Provenza*.[56] One list given by the Venetian Gioanventura Rosetti in his *Plictho* of 1548 is very similar, while in an earlier chapter he lists fewer varieties, including *grana di Armenia*.[57] This last could be Armenian cochineal, but in many other cases the names probably refer to the same species of insect gathered in different localities, varying in dyeing quality. The Arte della Seta document also lists two types of *chermisi*, *chermisi minuto* and *chermisi grosso*, while seven types of *cremesino* are listed in the *Plictho*. *Chermisi minuto*, at one florin a pound, was twice the price of *chermisi grosso* and the most expensive variety of *grana*, *grana di cintri*; the silks dyed with these insects were also dearer.[58] The carminic acid-containing insects, the Old and New World cochineals, give a bluer crimson or pink (depending on the depth of dyeing) than kermes (see Plate 1, p. 57) and it is possible that the term *chermisi* refers to varieties of these insects – perhaps even to different species, although not, at this date, to the Mexican insect.[59] The laborious harvesting of Polish cochineal, which occurs on the roots of

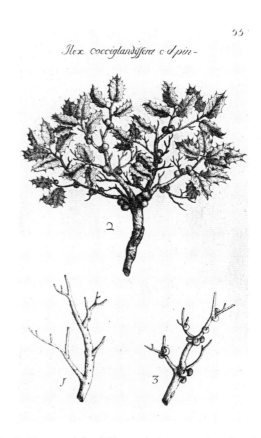

Fig. 3 *Ilex cocciglandiffera c.d.pin*: engraving showing kermes on its host, the kermes oak, from P.J. Garidel, *Histoire des plantes qui naissent aux environs d'Aix et des plusieurs autres endroits de la Provence*, 1715.[54] By permission of The British Library.

its host plant, usually the perennial knawel, *Scleranthus perennis* L. (Fig. 2), and the small size of the insect would undoubtedly contribute towards its expense as a source of colorant.

It is thus not surprising that scale insects and other dyestuffs were important items of trade; care was needed to choose good quality material. Pegolotti described how to examine *grana* by its weight and appearance and by chewing a sample; stick lac, *lacca*, both *matura* and *acerba*, is described in detail. He devoted almost as much attention to brazilwood and madder.[60] It is therefore understandable that shearings or clippings from expensive dyed textiles were re-used as a source of dyestuff, not only for pigments, but also in dyeing: the '*vlocken*' or '*bourre*' described in Northern European and French sources.[61] Lake pigment recipes describe how alkali was used to dissolve the dyestuff out of the textile waste; alum was then added to the coloured solution to precipitate the pigment. In fifteenth- or sixteenth-century recipes from the Netherlands and Germany, it appears that the alkali used was sufficiently strong to reduce the shearings to an amorphous, even gelatinous, consistency; it was deemed strong enough if it dissolved a feather.[62] Seventeenth-century descriptions of *bourre* in use seem rather similar.[63] In this case, the final pigment would contain much textile matter, not necessarily in a visually recognisable form. That this was not always so is evident from Italian recipes; in a typical example, from the fifteenth-century Bolognese manuscript, the alkaline dyestuff solution is pressed out of the textile fibres and the alkali is poured through again to extract more dyestuff. Clearly in this case the alkali used was less strong; a large part of the textile would remain in the filter.[64]

In a recent examination of Titian's *Venus and Adonis*, of about 1560, in the J. Paul Getty Museum, Malibu, microscopic examination of a cross-section prepared from a sample of the red glaze of the cloth draped over Venus' seat revealed the presence of a few textile fibres within the lake pigment, which contained both cochineal and madder dyestuffs.[65] While there are other possible explanations for the presence of the fibres (including the use of a piece of fabric to apply the paint or to level its surface),[66] the use of shearings in the preparation of the pigment is the most likely.

Plainly the precise dyestuff composition of a pigment so prepared would depend on that of the original textile matter, and thus also on that of the dyebath (or baths), its age, how many times it had been used and so forth. While it is not yet possible to throw much light on these factors, a clear connection between the preparation of lake pigments and textile dyeing may be demonstrated by the presence of a mixture of dyestuffs in a single pigment; there are, of course, several possible explanations for the presence of a mixture of dyestuffs in a sample of paint. It is quite common to find more than one layer of paint containing lake pigment and the lakes need not be the same. Yellow lake pigments may well occur unrecognised, mixed with other pigments, in layers of underpaint, quite apart from any possible admixture of yellow dyestuff with red dyestuff in a single lake pigment. This was found to be the case with several samples from paintings by Tintoretto in the Scuola di San Rocco, dating from the 1560s

to the 1580s; the red dyestuff used was cochineal (probably the New World insect in most cases), but the complexity of the paint structure has made the interpretation of the presence of the yellow dyestuff difficult.[67]

Artists sometimes mixed two lake pigments together to obtain the desired colour; this has been observed in a number of samples from seventeenth-century paintings, including several by Rembrandt, where a cochineal-containing red lake was mixed with a yellow lake to give a more orange red.[68] Thus, although mixtures of cochineal with yellow dyes, such as turmeric, were used in dyeing in Holland at this time,[69] the presence of a similar mixture in a paint sample does not necessarily indicate the use of shearings of textile dyed thus to prepare the lake pigment: turmeric is occasionally mentioned in cochineal lake recipes not employing shearings. Pigment recipes suggest also that, by this time, the links between pigment and textile were gradually becoming less close. Examination of the paint sample under the microscope could not reveal whether the mixture of dyestuffs (cochineal, probably, and madder) present in the thinly painted red glaze of Pax's drapery in Peter Paul Rubens's *Minerva protects Pax from Mars ('Peace and War')* (NG 46), painted in about 1629–30 (Table 2, p. 73), was due to the use of two lake pigments, mixed by the artist, or not. The fact that the picture was painted while the artist was in England is probably not significant (both dyestuffs were used in England at this time);[70] it is interesting, however, that the English artist William Larkin (died 1619) used a mixture of madder and cochineal lakes for certain passages in his *Portrait of Susan Villiers, Countess of Denbigh* (private collection), painted between 1610 and 1619. In other areas, cochineal lake was used alone.[71]

In several of the paintings examined, there is no indication that two lakes have been mixed; the dyestuffs are present in one pigment. Madder and kermes, for example, occur together in the pigment used for the robe of a courtier in *Saint Giles and the Hind* (NG 1419), painted by the Master of Saint Giles, probably in Paris in about 1500; kermes and a variety of cochineal are found together in Lorenzo Lotto's *Portrait of Giovanni della Volta and his Family(?)* (NG 1047; Plate 7) of about 1547 (Table 2, p. 71). The presence of a similar mixture in the lake used for the cloth of honour in David's *The Virgin and Child with Saints and a Donor* (NG 1432) has been discussed above. The use of textile shearings as a source for the dyestuff is the most likely explanation for such mixtures. Similar results were obtained from the group of sixteenth-century altarpieces from Antwerp mentioned above, where not only kermes mixed with madder, but also kermes mixed with redwood (brazilwood), were found.[72] Brazilwood was sometimes used in textile dyeing to modify the colour given by madder or kermes, sometimes in imitation of the colour given by a better quality dyestuff.[73] In the one occurrence identified (Table 2, p. 72), it occurs mixed with madder in the faded pink dress of the Virgin in *The Virgin and Child in a Landscape* (NG 713), an early sixteenth-century painting attributed to Jan Provoost. In practice one cannot be sure that a pigment containing a mixture of dyestuffs can be related directly to a single textile dyed with this mixture: shearings from more than one textile could have been used. However, mixtures of kermes and madder were widely used in, for example, the '*meza grana*' dyeings described by Rosetti and the '*demy-graines*' or '*demy-cramoisis*' of seventeenth-century France;[74] if the shearings were from one textile, the original dyeing could have been of this type. In many recipes for dyeing with scale insects, a proportion of better-quality insect matter ('*pococco*' or '*poppo*') is introduced into the bath, perhaps as a 'starting' material; there was plenty of opportunity for mixing of insects to occur as more dyestuff was added as necessary and the bath was re-used until exhausted.[75]

There are few references to the use of lac dyestuff in textile dyeing in the fifteenth and sixteenth centuries; the results of analysis show that as a lake pigment it occurred widely over a long period. Pegolotti and others describe stick lac's tubular form, colour and grainy appearance very fully, while being unaware of its animal origins;[76] the 'large ants' that 'deposit the lacre' were first described to a European audience in 1563 by the Portuguese physician Garcia da Orta.[77] By the latter part of the seventeenth century the raw material was imported into Europe in large quantity by the English and the Dutch, but as much for the resin-like component which is the source of shellac as for the dyestuff. By

the end of the eighteenth century, the crudely separated dyestuff was imported into England from India in the form of cakes of 'lac lake', of very variable composition, according to Edward Bancroft. His detailed account tells nothing of its use in Europe in the fifteenth century and earlier, however: he and other contemporary writers seem to have been largely unaware of this.[78] Too few results have been obtained from paintings dating from the mid-sixteenth century onwards to throw light on the later history of the use of the pigment in easel painting; one cannot say if the use of lac lake by Philippe de Champaigne in his portrait of Cardinal Richelieu (Plate 4) represents a relatively late occurrence or not. Certainly, fifty years later, French lake pigment recipes concentrate on cochineal – notably cochineal carmine – and brazilwood; Pierre Mignard used a cochineal lake in his painting *The Marquise de Seignelay and Two of her Children* (NG 2967) of 1691 (Table 2, p. 73).[79]

It appears that lac lake was the 'standard' lake used for easel painting in the fifteenth century in Florence, and probably other parts of Italy as well. Examples of its use are seen in paintings by four Florentine painters, Filippino Lippi, Domenico and David Ghirlandaio and Michelangelo (NG 1412, 3937, 2502 and 809), the subject in each case being a variant of the Virgin and Child theme, illustrated in Plates 3, 5, 6 and 7, on pp. 22–3 of this *Bulletin*.[80] In Filippino Lippi's painting, lac lake was used for the glaze on Saint John's cloak; in the paintings by Domenico Ghirlandaio and Michelangelo it was used for the dress of the Virgin, traces of kermes lake also being present. In David Ghirlandaio's painting lac lake was used to glaze red areas of the carpet, while the Virgin's dress was painted with kermes lake mixed with a little lac lake. Italian documentary sources of the fifteenth and sixteenth centuries generally refer to *lacca* and *lacca di cimatura*. Paolo Bensi, in an article on the Florentine Confraternità dei Gesuati of the Convent of San Giusto alle Mura, who supplied good quality pigments to painters during the second half of the fifteenth century, has suggested that the former referred to lac lake, while the latter referred to a lake prepared from shearings of cloth dyed, probably, with kermes.[81] The results of analysis obtained so far suggest that this is likely to be the case. Examination of the accounts of the Florentine painter Neri di Bicci indicate that, while *lacca* was expensive at 14 *soldi* an ounce in about 1466–71 (compared with 3 *soldi* for an ounce of the yellow lake pigment *arzica* and 4 *soldi* a pound for lead white), *lacca di cimatura* was perhaps about twice that price; only ultramarine and good quality azurite were dearer.[82] This was still the case nearly a century later in Venice: Lorenzo Lotto, who used what was probably a lake prepared from shearings in the *Portrait of Giovanni della Volta and his Family(?)* (NG 1047; Plate 7), paid 2 *lire* 15 *soldi* for an ounce of *lacca di grana* in 1542, but only 4 *soldi* for a pound of lead white.[83] In easel painting cost thus played a part in which pigment was used; in manuscript illumination this would be a less important factor, as the identification of a Polish cochineal lake – perhaps prohibitively expensive for use in most easel paintings – in a fifteenth-century Sienese manuscript suggests.[84] The presence of traces of one lake mixed with the other (most notably in the Virgin's dress in David Ghirlandaio's painting) could be explained by a desire not to waste expensive pigment, as much as for any reason of colour.

With the arrival of the dyestuff-rich New World cochineal insect in Europe, the use of kermes as a source of dye declined. By the mid-eighteenth century it was used for dyeing in Venice, according to Jean Hellot, while in France it was barely used at all; by the late nineteenth century the quantity used in Europe was negligible.[85] It remained available, however; like several of the materials used as sources of dyestuff, it had medicinal value. It has astringent properties and was also used to prepare a cordial (and subsequently a syrup) derived from the famous *Confectio Alkermes*, devised in the ninth century by the Arabic physician Mesue. This panacea was popular even into the nineteenth century.[86]

If kermes was used for dyeing, even on a small scale, there is no reason why the preparation of kermes lakes should not also have continued here and there. Recipes for kermes lake appear in some early nineteenth-century sources and George Field was given samples of French kermes lakes, although at the time he doubted their authenticity.[87] Kermes was identified in the lake pigment used for the Virgin's

Plate 7 Lorenzo Lotto, *Portrait of Giovanni della Volta and his Family (?)* (NG 1047), probably 1547. Canvas, 114.9 × 139.7 cm.

red dress in Boltraffio's *Virgin and Child* (NG 728), painted in Milan probably around 1493–9. The dress is one area of the painting known to have been repainted completely, probably before it left Italy in 1854;[88] this is thus a very late occurrence of a pigment which must have become difficult to obtain outside areas (such as Venice or Montpellier) where kermes still had some specialist uses. During the first thirty years or so of the nineteenth century, the improvement in methods of extracting madder dyestuff, following the work of Colin and Robiquet in France and Field and others in England, had resulted in greatly improved madder pigments; these, with cochineal pigments, became the artists' colours of choice until the final years of the century.

Acknowledgements

The authors are most grateful to Colin Harvey and Astrid Athen of the Photographic Department for Plate 1, to Marika Spring for the photomicrographs used in Plates 2a and b, to Dr Lorne Campbell, Courtauld Institute, University of London, for his assistance with translation of the Early Netherlandish texts, and to Penelope Walton Rogers, of Textile Research Associates, York, for copies of certain references.

Table 2 Lake Pigment Dyestuffs

Artist	Title of Painting	Date	Sample	Dyestuff
ITALIAN SCHOOLS				
Lorenzo Monaco	*Adoring Saints* NG 216	probably 1407–9	Red robe of saint on left holding book, left-hand edge	Probably kermes[89]
Fra Angelico, Follower	*The Annunciation* NG 1406	c.1434	Crimson shadow of fold in angel's robe	Kermes
			Crimson glaze of roundel decoration on Virgin's dress	Kermes (possibly + lac)
Paolo Uccello	*The Battle of San Romano* NG 583	probably c.1450–60	Wine-red plume of helmet of foreground figure	Probably lac
Giovanni di Paolo	*Saints Fabian and Sebastian* NG 3402	c.1475–82	Saint Fabian's red robe	Kermes, probably + a little lac[90]
Filippino Lippi	*The Virgin and Child with Saint John* NG 1412	c.1475–80	Red of Saint John's cloak	Lac
Domenico Ghirlandaio	*The Virgin and Child* NG 3937	probably c.1480–90	Mid-pink glaze of Virgin's dress	Probably lac (possibly + kermes)
David Ghirlandaio	*The Virgin and Child with Saint John* NG 2502	probably c.1480–90	Red glaze of carpet	Lac
			Red glaze of Virgin's dress	Kermes (possibly + lac)
Filippino Lippi, Follower	*The Worship of the Egyptian Bull God, Apis* NG 4905	c.1500	Brownish-red robe of man on left with blue headdress, shadow of fold	Probably kermes[91]
Carlo Crivelli	*The Immaculate Conception* NG 906	1492	Mauvish glaze of cloth of honour	Probably kermes
Michelangelo	*The Virgin and Child with Saint John and Angels* ('The Manchester Madonna') NG 809	c.1497	Crimson shadow of fold in Virgin's dress	Principally lac
Francesco Bissolo	*The Virgin and Child with Saints Michael and Veronica and Two Donors* NG 3083	probably 1500–25	Red of Saint Veronica's dress	Kermes
Francesco Zaganelli	*The Baptism of Christ* NG 3892.1	1514	Saint John the Baptist's red drapery, shadow of fold	Kermes
Bacchiacca	*Joseph pardons his Brothers* NG 1219	probably 1515	Deep crimson of coat lining of figure with straw hat, left foreground	Kermes

Artist	Title of Painting	Date	Sample	Dyestuff
Altobello Melone	*The Walk to Emmaus* NG 753	*c.*1516–20	Red of Christ's robe	Kermes
	Christ carrying the Cross NG 6546	*c.*1520–5	Red of Christ's robe	Madder
Garofalo	*The Holy Family with Saints John the Baptist, Elizabeth, Zacharias and (?)Francis* NG 170	*c.*1520	Shadow in fold of Virgin's red dress	Lac
Vincenzo Catena	*Portrait of the Doge, Andrea Gritti* NG 5751	probably 1523–31	Red glaze on cap	Kermes
			Pink of sitter's right sleeve	Kermes
Lorenzo Lotto	*Portrait of Giovanni della Volta and his Family (?)* NG 1047	probably 1547	Deep red shadow in fold of woman's skirt	Kermes + trace of cochineal
Paolo Veronese	*The Consecration of Saint Nicholas* NG 26	1561–2	Red collar of figure in white cassock	Cochineal, probably Polish cochineal[92]
	Allegory of Love, I ('Unfaithfulness') NG 1318	probably 1570s	Deepest red shadow of tunic of man, left	Cochineal, probably the New World insect[93]
			Mid-tone of red drapery of man, left	Cochineal, probably the New World insect
			Reddish-brown shadow on orange tunic of man, right	Cochineal, probably the New World insect
	Allegory of Love, IV ('Happy Union') NG 1326	probably 1570s	Red of brocade dress, shadow, bottom edge	Cochineal, probably the New World insect
	The Adoration of the Kings NG 268	1573	Shadow of red drapery of kneeling king	Cochineal, probably Polish cochineal
Tintoretto	*The Origin of the Milky Way* NG 1313	probably 1575–80	Red drapery upon which Venus is seated	Lac[94]
Palma Giovane	*Mars and Venus* NG 1866	probably 1585–90	Shadow of red curtain, upper left corner	Cochineal (source unclear)
Neapolitan School	*The Adoration of the Shepherds* NG 232	probably 1630s	Red of Virgin's dress	Cochineal (New World)[95]
After **Guido Reni**	*Perseus and Andromeda* NG 87	1635–1700	Red drapery near Andromeda's hip	Cochineal[96]
Giovanni Antonio Pellegrini	*Rebecca at the Well* NG 6332	1708–13	Servant's red cloak, from lower left corner	Cochineal (New World)
Canaletto	*A Regatta on the Grand Canal* NG 4454	*c.*1740	Red of textile	Cochineal (New World)
SPANISH SCHOOL				
Diego Velázquez	*Portrait of Archbishop Fernando de Valdés* NG 6380	1640–5	Red glaze of curtain	Cochineal (probably New World)

Artist	Title of Painting	Date	Sample	Dyestuff
EARLY NETHERLANDISH SCHOOLS				
Rogier van der Weyden and Workshop	*The Exhumation of Saint Hubert* NG 783	*c*.1440	Red robe of figure on extreme left	Probably madder
Dieric Bouts	*The Virgin and Child with Saints Peter and Paul* NG 774	probably 1460s	Reddish-purple of Saint Paul's robe	Madder
Dieric Bouts, Workshop	*Christ crowned with Thorns* NG 712	probably 1475–1500	Red of Christ's robe	Madder
Netherlandish School	*The Virgin and Child with Saints and Angels in a Garden* NG 1085 Central Panel: *Mystic Marriage of Saint Catherine*	*c*.1500	Red glaze of fold of dress of woman, right	Probably kermes[97]
Master of Saint Giles	*Saint Giles and the Hind* NG 1419	*c*.1500	Red of courtier's robe, left-hand edge	Madder + kermes[98]
After Quinten Massys	*Christ* NG 295.1	probably *c*.1500–50	Wine-red of Christ's sleeve	Madder
Attributed to Jan Provoost	*The Virgin and Child in a Landscape* NG 713	early 16th century	Pink of Virgin's cloak	Brazilwood + madder
Gerard David	*The Virgin and Child with Saints and Donor* NG 1432	probably 1510	Purple of cloth of honour	Kermes + cochineal (Old World insect source)
Ambrosius Benson	*The Magdalen Reading* NG 655	*c*.1525	Red of the Magdalen's robe	Kermes + trace cochineal
GERMAN SCHOOLS				
Stephan Lochner	*Saints Matthew, Catherine of Alexandria and John the Evangelist* NG 705. Reverse: *Saint Jerome, a female martyr, Saint Gregory the Great and a Donor*	*c*.1445	Red glaze of Saint Jerome's pinkish-red cloak	Probably kermes
Master of Liesborn	*Saints Cosmas and Damian and the Virgin* NG 261	probably 1470–80	Red glaze of Saint Damian's robe, bottom edge	Probably madder
Attributed to the Master of Liesborn	*The Crucifixion with Saints* NG 262	*c*.1465–90	Red glaze of drapery, second figure from left	Probably madder
Master of the Aachen Altarpiece	*The Crucifixion* NG 1049	*c*.1495–1505	Red glaze of skirt of kneeling woman left, from left-hand edge	Probably largely kermes[99]
Attributed to Albrecht Dürer	*The Painter's Father* NG 1938	1497	Pink background, left-hand edge (after extraction of paint medium)	Madder
Master of the Saint Bartholomew Altarpiece	*Saints Peter and Dorothy* NG 707. Reverse: *Saint John the Evangelist and the Virgin and Child*	probably 1505–10	Red glaze of shadow on Saint John's left sleeve	Probably madder[100]

Artist	Title of Painting	Date	Sample	Dyestuff
Hans Holbein the Younger	'The Ambassadors' NG 1314	1533	Pink of Jean de Dinteville's left sleeve	Lac[101]
DUTCH SCHOOL				
Hendrick ter Brugghen	Jacob reproaching Laban for giving him Leah in place of Rachel NG 4164	1627	Red glaze of Jacob's waist band	Cochineal (New World)
Rembrandt, Follower	A Young Man and a Girl playing Cards NG 1247	perhaps c.1645–50	Red glaze of girl's skirt	Cochineal (New World)[102]
Jan Jansz. Treck	Vanitas Still Life NG 6533	1648	Shadow on red stripe of cloth	Cochineal (source unclear)
FLEMISH SCHOOL				
Anthony van Dyck	Charity NG 6494	c.1627–8	Cherry-coloured glaze of drapery, from left-hand edge	Cochineal (source unclear)
Peter Paul Rubens	Minerva protects Pax from Mars ('Peace and War') NG 46	1629–30	Glaze on Pax's red drapery	Probably cochineal + madder[103]
FRENCH SCHOOL				
Master of Moulins (Jean Hey)	Charlemagne, and the Meeting of Saints Joachim and Anne at the Golden Gate NG 4092	c.1500	Glaze of Joachim's red hat	Madder
			Charlemagne's pink cloak	Probably madder
Philippe de Champaigne	Cardinal Richelieu NG 1449	c.1637	Shadow in fold of dark red robe (after extraction of paint medium)	Lac
Pierre Mignard	The Marquise de Seignelay and Two of her Children NG 2967	1691	Red drapery of younger child, right	Cochineal (New World)
Maurice-Quentin de La Tour	Henry Dawkins NG 5118	c.1750	Red coat, from lower edge	Cochineal (New World)[104]
Paul Delaroche	The Execution of Lady Jane Grey NG 1909	1833	Red glaze of brocade dress on attendant's lap	Cochineal (New World)[105]
			Red glaze of shadow on executioner's calf	Cochineal (New World)
Gustave Moreau	Saint George and the Dragon NG 6436	1889–90	Red drapery falling across horse's back	Cochineal (New World)
ENGLISH SCHOOL				
Sir Joshua Reynolds	Anne, Countess of Albemarle NG 1259	probably 1759–60	Red glaze on curtain, left-hand side	Cochineal (probably New World)[106]
Thomas Gainsborough	Mrs Siddons NG 683	c.1783–5	Red of shawl, right-hand side	Cochineal (New World)[107]
Sir Thomas Lawrence	Queen Charlotte NG 4257	1789–90	Glaze on brownish-red foliage, left-hand edge	Probably cochineal (New World)
Joseph Mallord William Turner	Ulysses deriding Polyphemus NG 508	1829	Red of edge of ship	Cochineal (New World)

Notes and References

1. H. Davy, 'Some experiments and observations on the colours used in painting by the Ancients', *Philosophical Transactions of the Royal Society*, 105, 1815, pp. 97–124, especially pp. 113–16.

2. Davy, ibid., pp. 99–100, 115. See also J. Chaptal, 'Sur quelques couleurs trouvées à Pompeia', *Annales de chimie*, 70, 1809, pp. 22–31.

3. J. Kirby, 'The Preparation of Early Lake Pigments: A Survey', *Dyes on Historical and Archaeological Textiles*, 6, 1987, pp. 12–18 (renamed *Dyes in History and Archaeology* from Vol. 7 onwards); I. Stössel, *Rote Farblacke in der Malerei: Herstellung und Verwendung im deutschsprachigen Raum zwischen ca.1400 und 1850*, Diplomarbeit, Institut für Technologie der Malerei der Staatlichen Akademie der Bildenden Künste, Stuttgart 1985. For the history, biology and general use of the dyes see F. Brunello, *L'Arte della tintura nella storia dell'umanità*, Vicenza 1968 (English edn. Vicenza 1973); D. Cardon, *Guide des teintures naturelles: plantes, lichens, champignons, mollusques et insectes*, Neuchâtel 1990; D. Cardon, *Les 'vers' du rouge: insectes tinctoriaux (Homoptera: Coccoidea) utilisés dans l'Ancien Monde au Moyen-Age*, Paris 1990 (Cahiers d'Histoire et de Philosophie des Sciences, n.s. no. 28, produced by the Société Française d'Histoire des Sciences et des Techniques); R.A. Donkin, 'The Insect Dyes of Western and West Central Asia', *Anthropos: International Review of Ethnology and Linguistics*, 72, 1977, pp. 847–80; R.A. Donkin, 'Spanish Red: An Ethnographical Study of Cochineal and the Opuntia Cactus', *Transactions of the American Philosophical Society (N.S.)*, 67, 5, 1977, pp. 5–84; H. Schweppe, *Handbuch der Naturfarbstoffe; Vorkommen; Verwendung; Nachweis*, Landsberg/ Lech 1993; A. Verhecken and J. Wouters, 'The Coccid Insect Dyes: Historical, Geographical and Technical Data', *Bulletin de l'Institut Royal du Patrimoine Artistique*, XXII, 1988/89, pp. 207–39.

4. Habotai medium weight silk, supplied by Whaleys (Bradford) Ltd, was dyed using a mordant of aluminium potassium sulphate, $AlK(SO_4)_2.12H_2O$ (25%). The wool used was $6^{1}/_{2}$ cut KB undyed, oiled, supplied by J. Hyslop Bathgate & Co., Galashiels. The oil was removed by scouring in Decon 90; the wool was then rinsed well and a mordant of 8% aluminium potassium sulphate, 7% potassium hydrogen tartrate, $KO_2CCH(OH)CH(OH)CO_2H$, was used for dyeing: see G. Dalby, *Natural Dyes, Fast or Fugitive*, Alcombe 1985, for method. The preparation of the pigments is discussed in J. Kirby, 'A Spectrophotometric Method for the Identification of Lake Pigment Dyestuffs', *National Gallery Technical Bulletin*, 1, 1977, pp. 35–45, especially pp. 37–8, and D. Saunders and J. Kirby, 'Light-induced Colour Changes in Red and Yellow Lake Pigments', *National Gallery Technical Bulletin*, 15, 1994, pp. 79–97, especially pp. 83–4, 96–7. The kermes lake illustrated was prepared from clippings of dyed wool.

5. A. Wallert, '"Cimatura de grana": Identification of Natural Organic Colorants and Binding Media in Mediaeval Manuscript Illumination', *Zeitschrift für Kunsttechnologie und Konservierung*, 5, 1, 1991, pp. 74–83.

6. J.S. Remington and W. Francis, *Pigments: Their Manufacture, Properties and Use*, London 1954, pp. 193–4.

7. For example, see M. Saltzman, 'The Identification of Dyes in Archaeological and Ethnographic Textiles', *Archaeological Chemistry*, II; edited by G.F. Carter, Washington 1978, pp. 172–85; M. Saltzman, A.M. Keay and J. Christensen, 'The Identification of Colorants in Ancient Textiles', *Dyestuffs*, 44, 8, 1963, pp. 241–51; M. Whiting, 'The Identification of Dyes in Old Oriental Textiles', *ICOM Committee for Conservation, 5th Triennial Meeting, Zagreb, 1–8 October, 1978: Preprints*, Zagreb 1978, pp. 78/9/2/1–9; R. Kumar, F.W. Billmeyer, Jr, and M. Saltzman, 'Identification of Organic Pigments in Paints', *Journal of Coatings Technology*, 57, 1985, pp. 49–54. (The paper discusses the application of the method to modern synthetic pigments.)

8. A. Wallert, 'Fluorescent assay of quinone, lichen and redwood dyestuffs', *Studies in Conservation*, 31, 1986, pp. 145–55.

9. Wallert, 1991, cited in note 5.

10. N.F. Barnes, 'A Spectrophotometric Study of Artists' Pigments', *Technical Studies in the Field of the Fine Arts*, VII, 3, 1939, pp. 120–38; D.R. Duncan, 'The Identification and Estimation of Pigments in Pigmented Compositions by Reflectance Spectrophotometry', *Journal of the Oil and Colour Chemists' Association*, 45, 1962, pp. 300–24; B. Guineau, 'Non-destructive analysis of organic pigments and dyes using Raman microprobe, microfluorometer or absorption microspectrophotometer', *Studies in Conservation*, 34, 1989, pp. 38–44; D.R. Cousins, C.R. Platoni and L.W. Russell, 'The use of microspectrophotometry for the identification of pigments in small paint samples', *Forensic Science International*, 24, 1984, pp. 183–96; C. Binant, 'Application de la microspectrophotométrie de réflexion diffuse à l'analyse de pigments de quinacridones', *Pigments et colorants de l'Antiquité et du Moyen Age* (proceedings of an international colloquium of the Centre National de la Recherche Scientifique, Orléans, 5-8 December 1988), Paris 1990, pp. 156–62.

11. Kirby, 1977, cited in note 4. The method is still in use with modified equipment.

12. B. Guineau, 'Experiments in the identification of colorants *in situ*: possibilities and limitations', *Dyes in History and Archaeology*, 10, 1991, pp. 55–9.

13. S. Shimoyama and Y. Noda, 'Non-destructive Determination of Natural Dyestuffs used for Ancient Coloured Cloths using a Three-Dimensional Fluorescence Spectrum Technique', *Dyes in History and Archaeology*, 12, 1993, pp. 45–56.

14. M.J.D. Low and N.S. Baer, 'Application of infrared Fourier transform spectroscopy to problems in conservation', *Studies in Conservation*, 22, 1977, pp. 116–28; R.D. Gillard, S.M. Hardman, R.G. Thomas and D.E. Watkinson, 'The detection of dyes by FTIR microscopy', *Studies in Conservation*, 39, 1994, pp. 187–92.

15. W.G.Th. Roelofs, P.H. Hallebeek, J.H. Hofenk de Graaff and R.F.S. Karreman, 'The analysis of natural dyestuffs and organic pigments: A comparative study into the possibilities and limits of various methods', *ICOM Committee for Conservation, 8th Triennial Meeting, Sydney, Australia, 6–11 September, 1987: Preprints*, edited by K. Grimstad, Malibu 1987, pp. 709–17.

16. Jennifer Pilc has commented that during examination of paint samples by FTIR alizarin crimson in retouchings can often be detected, whereas it is rarely possible to gather any useful information on lake pigment dyestuffs in the original paint.

17. See, for example, S.P. Best, R.J.H. Clark and R. Withnall, 'Non-destructive pigment analysis of artefacts by Raman microscopy', *Endeavour*, n.s. 16, 2, 1992, pp. 66–73; S.P. Best, R.J.H. Clark, M.A.M. Daniels, C.A. Porter and R. Withnall, 'Identification by Raman microscopy and visible reflectance spectroscopy of pigments on an Icelandic manuscript', *Studies in Conservation*, 40, 1995, pp. 31–40.

18. B. Guineau, 'Analyse non destructive des pigments par microsonde Raman laser: exemples de l'azurite et de la malachite', *Studies in Conservation*, 29, 1984, pp. 35–41; B. Guineau and V. Guichard, 'Identification de colorants organiques naturels par microspectrometrie Raman de résonance et par effet Raman exalté de surface (SERS); exemple d'application à l'étude de tranchefiles de reliures anciennes teintes à la garance', *ICOM Committee for Conservation, 8th Triennial Meeting*, cited in note 15, pp. 659–66; V. Guichard and B. Guineau, 'Identification de colorants organiques naturels dans les fragments de peintures murales de l'Antiquité. Exemples de l'emploi d'une laque rose de garance à Stabies et à Vaison-la-Romaine', *Pigments et colorants de l'Antiquité et du Moyen Age*, cited in note 10, pp. 245–54.

19. L. Masschelein-Kleiner, 'Microanalysis of hydroxyquinones in red lakes', *Mikrochimica Acta*, 6, 1967, pp. 1080–5; J.H. Hofenk-de Graaff, *Natural Dyestuffs: Origin, Chemical Constitution, Identification; International Council of Museums, Committee for Conservation, Plenary Meeting, September 15–19, 1969*, Amsterdam 1969; J.H. Hofenk-de Graaff and W.G.Th. Roelofs, *On the Occurrence of Red Dyestuffs in Textile Materials from the Period 1450–1600; International Council of Museums, Committee for Conservation, Plenary Meeting, October 2–5, 1972*, Madrid 1972; H. Schweppe, 'Identification of Dyes in Historic Textile Materials', *Historic Textile and Paper Materials: Conservation and Characterisation*, edited by H.L. Needles and S.H. Zeronian, American Chemical Society Symposium Series no. 212, Washington 1986, pp. 153–74; H. Schweppe, 'Identification of Red Madder and Insect Dyes by Thin-Layer Chromatography', *Historic Textile and Paper Materials, II: Conservation and Characterisation*, edited by S.H. Zeronian and H.L. Needles, American Chemical Society Symposium Series no. 410, Washington 1989, pp. 188–219.

20. Stössel, 1985, cited in note 3, pp. 128–39; *A Closer Look: Technical and Art-Historical Studies on Works by Van Gogh and Gauguin*, edited by C. Peres, M. Hoyle and L. van Tilborgh, Zwolle 1991; the results of examination of lake pigments used by Vincent van Gogh, by J.H. Hofenk de Graaff and others, are described on pp. 75–85; N. Eastaugh, 'Chromatography and Art History', *Chromatography and Analysis*, 19, October 1991, pp. 5–7; see also J.H. Townsend, 'The materials of J.M.W. Turner: pigments', *Studies in Conservation*, 38, 1993, pp. 231–54.

21. C. Walker and H.L. Needles, 'Analysis of Natural Dyes on Wool Substrates Using Reverse-Phase High Performance Liquid Chromatography', *Historic Textile and Paper Materials: Conservation and Characterisation*, 1986, cited in note 19, pp. 175–85; J. Wouters, 'High performance liquid chromatography of anthraquinones: analysis of plant and insect extracts and dyed textiles', *Studies in Conservation*, 30, 1985, pp. 119–28; J. Wouters and A. Verhecken, 'The coccid insect dyes: HPLC and computerised diode-array analysis of dyed yarns', *Studies in Conservation*, 34, 1989, pp. 189–200.

22. J. Wouters and A. Verhecken, 'The scale insect dyes (*Homoptera: Coccoidea*). Species recognition by HPLC and diode-array analysis of the dyestuffs', *Annales de la Société Entomologique de France*, (N.S.) 25, 4, 1989, pp. 393–410; J. Wouters and A. Verhecken,

'Potential Taxonomic Applications of H.P.L.C. Analysis of Coccoidea Pigments (Homoptera: Sternorhyncha)', *Belgian Journal of Zoology*, 121, 2, 1991, pp. 211–25.

23. J. Wouters, 'Dyestuff Analysis of Scale Insects by High Performance Liquid Chromatography (Homoptera: Coccoidea)', *Proceedings of ISSIS-VI (Krakov)*, Part II, 1990, pp. 61–70.

24. J. Sanyova and J. Wouters, 'Painting Techniques of Polychromed Antwerp Altarpieces', *Dyes in History and Archaeology*, 12, 1993, pp. 36–44 (see also J. Sanyova, 'Etude scientifique des techniques picturales des retables anversois', *Antwerpse retabels, 15de–16de eeuw*, exhibition catalogue, edited by H. Nieuwdorp, 2 vols., Antwerp 1993, Vol. II, pp. 151–64); P.W.F. Brinkman, L. Kockaert, L. Maes, E.M.M. Thielen and J. Wouters, 'Het Lam Godsretabel van van Eyck: een heronderzoek naar de materialen en schildermethoden. 2. De hoofdkleuren: blauw, groen, geel en rood', *Bulletin de l'Institut Royal du Patrimoine Artistique*, XXII, 1988/89, pp. 26–49, especially p. 38; J. Wouters, 'Materials and Techniques: Organic Lakes', *Peter Paul Rubens's Elevation of the Cross: Study, Examination and Treatment, Bulletin de l'Institut Royal du Patrimoine Artistique*, XXIV, 1992, p. 82.

25. Wouters, 1990, cited in note 23, p. 62; using the computerised diode-array detector, the limit of detection claimed is 10ng carminic acid, compared with about 100ng carminic acid for the system described.

26. Wouters and Verhecken, 1989, cited in note 22, p. 394.

27. Schweppe, 1989, cited in note 19, pp. 201–2; Wouters and Verhecken, 1989, cited in note 21, p. 190.

28. *Handbook of Derivatives for Chromatography*; edited by K. Blau and J. Halket, 2nd edn., Chichester 1993, p. 15.

29. R. White and J. Pilc, 'Analyses of Paint Media', in this *Bulletin*, p. 95.

30. The taxonomy of lac insects is complex; the *Kerria lacca* Kerr group is the commonest and most widely distributed, occurring in India, Pakistan, Nepal and Sri Lanka. The *Kerria greeni* Chamberlin group of species occurs in Burma, Indonesia, Malaysia and Australia. See R.K. Varshney, 'A Review of the Family Tachardiidae (Kerriidae) in the Orient (Homoptera: Coccoidea)', *Oriental Insects*, 18, 1984, pp. 361–84.

31. The standards used in the National Gallery laboratory were supplied by Professor K. Schofield of Exeter University, are labelled A_1 and B, and are impure: see R. Burwood, G. Read, K. Schofield and D.E. Wright, 'The Pigments of Stick Lac. Part I. Isolation and Preliminary Examination', *Journal of the Chemical Society*, 1965, pp. 6067–73; R. Burwood et al., 'The Pigments of Stick Lac. Part II. The Structure of Laccaic acid A_1', *Journal of the Chemical Society (C)*, 1967, pp. 842–51. The structure of laccaic acid A elucidated by Professor Venkataraman's group at the National Chemical Laboratory, Poona, is identical to A_1; the same group have published the structure for laccaic acid B, but unfortunately could not supply the authors with any for use as a standard. See E.D. Pandhare, A.V. Rama Rao and I.N. Shaik, 'Lac Pigments: Part III – Isolation of Laccaic Acids A and B and the Constitution of Laccaic Acid A', *Indian Journal of Chemistry*, 7, 1969, pp. 977–86; N.S. Bhide, E.D. Pandhare, A.V. Rama Rao, I.N. Shaik and R. Srinivasan, 'Lac Pigments: Part IV – Constitution of Laccaic Acid B', ibid., pp. 987–95.

32. M. Wyld, A. Roy and A. Smith, 'Gerard David's "The Virgin and Child with Saints and a Donor"', *National Gallery Technical Bulletin*, 3, 1979, pp. 51–65, especially p. 62; Donkin, 'Spanish Red: An Ethnographical Study of Cochineal and the Opuntia Cactus', 1977, cited in note 3, pp. 23–4, 37.

33. J. Wouters, 'Een norm voor HPLC analyse van natuurlijke kleurstoffen: een noodzaak voor analyst en textielconservator, *Bulletin de l'Institut Royal du Patrimoine Artistique*, XXIII, 1990/91, pp. 213–20. The preparation of lake pigments for use as standards is discussed in Kirby, 1977, cited in note 4, pp. 37–8, and Saunders and Kirby, 1994, cited in note 4, pp. 83–4, 96–7.

34. *The Flavonoids*, ed. J.B. Harborne, T.J. Mabry and H. Mabry, London 1975, pp. 817, 853–4; Schweppe, 1993, cited in note 3, pp. 412–16, 420–1. For the chemistry of the anthraquinone dyestuffs, see R.H. Thomson, *Naturally Occurring Quinones*, 2nd edn., London 1971, and *Naturally Occurring Quinones III: Recent Advances*, London 1987 (the 3rd edn. updates, but does not replace the 2nd.).

35. For the laccaic acid standards see note 31 above. Alizarin, purpurin and carminic acid were supplied by Aldrich Chemical Co. Ltd, Gillingham, Dorset. Flavokermesic acid was supplied by Dr J. Wouters, Koninklijk Instituut voor het Kunstpatrimonium, Brussels. Kermesic acid was identified by UV-visible spectroscopy.

36. Pseudopurpurin, 1,2,4-trihydroxyanthraquinone-3-carboxylic acid, is present in the root, largely in the form of galiosin (pseudopurpurin-1-ß-D-primveroside), which may be responsible for a peak eluted at about 139 minutes. It may be converted to purpurin by decarboxylation as the ground root is stored and exposed to the air. Schweppe, 1993, cited in note 3, pp. 230, 240; ibid., 1989, cited in note 19, pp. 193, 201–3.

37. R.K. Varshney, 'Taxonomic Studies on Lac Insects of India', *Oriental Insects*, Supplement 5, 1976, pp. 1–97, especially pp. 42–3; M.E. Ali, D.C. Das, M.I.H. Khan and K. Ahmed, 'Investigation on Lac. Part V. Effect on the Composition of Lac due to Change of Host Plants of Lac Insect', *Bangladesh Journal of Scientific and Industrial Research*, 14, 1–2, 1979, pp. 286–8.

38. Wouters and Verhecken, 1989, cited in note 22; A.R. Burnett and R.H. Thomson, 'Naturally Occurring Quinones. Part XV. Biogenesis of the Anthraquinones in *Rubia tinctorum* L. (Madder)', *Journal of the Chemical Society* (C), 1968, pp. 2437–41.

39. J.P. Breynius, *Historia naturalis cocci radicum tinctorii, quod polonicum vulgo audit; praemissis quibusdam coccum in genere et in specie coccum ex ilice, quod grana kermes et alterum Americanum, quod cochinilla hispanis dicitur spectantibus*, Gdansk 1731, plates and caption (unnumbered) at end of text.

40. G. Taylor, 'Insect Red Dyes: An Update', *Dyes on Historical and Archaeological Textiles*, 6, 1987, pp. 21–4; Wouters and Verhecken, 1989, cited in note 22, pp. 400–2, 407. For the distribution of the principal Old World cochineal insects see Donkin, 'The Insect Dyes of Western and West Central Asia', 1977, cited in note 3, p. 848. There are other, less well-known, Old World scale insects found in parts of Eastern Europe and the Near East which may have been used locally for dyeing: see Cardon, *Guide des teintures naturelles*, 1990, cited in note 3, pp. 361–2, 377–8; Wouters and Verhecken, 1991, cited in note 22, p. 21.

41. Wouters and Verhecken, 1989, cited in note 22, pp. 402–4, 406–7.

42. Brazilwood was tentatively identified in one sample, from the striped sash of a woman on the extreme left of Veronese's *The Family of Darius before Alexander* (NG 294), dated 1565–70, by TLC in 1977 and microspectrophotometry in 1994. Microspectrophotometric examination of other samples of red lake pigment from the painting suggested the presence of a scale insect dyestuff; in other works by Veronese in the National Gallery cochineal-containing lakes have been found, as Table 2 shows. See N. Penny and M. Spring, 'Veronese's Paintings in the National Gallery. Technique and Materials: Part I', *National Gallery Technical Bulletin*, 16, 1995, pp. 4–29, especially pp. 21–2.

43. Hofenk-de Graaff and Roelofs, 1972, cited in note 19, p. 25. It is clear that the dyestuff was considered to be of lower quality, however much it may have been used. The statutes of the Venetian dyers' guild of 1243 include a stricture against its use without permission; a similar stricture (also applying to madder) appears in the statutes of the Lucca dyers' guild of 1255. This is a typical example of a prohibition against the substitution of a cheaper material for a more expensive one: in the Florentine painters' guild regulations of 1315–16, for example, the substitution of azurite for ultramarine is forbidden. Brazilwood's poor light-fastness would have been one factor behind the regulation. See Brunello, 1968, cited in note 3, pp. 140–4; D. Bomford, J. Dunkerton, D. Gordon, A. Roy and J. Kirby, *Art in the Making: Italian Painting before 1400*, London 1989, pp. 6–7, 213–14.

44. W. Cholmeley, 'The Request and Suite of a True-Hearted Englishman, written by William Cholmeley, Londyner, in the year 1553', edited by W.J. Thomas, in *Tudor Economic Documents*, edited by R.H. Tawney and E. Power, 3 vols., London 1924 (1951 reprint), Vol. III, no. 5, pp. 130–48, especially pp. 137, 139.

45. Hofenk-de Graaff and Roelofs, 1972, cited in note 19; W.G.Th. Roelofs and J.H. Hofenk de Graaff, 'Analisi delle materie coloranti', *Botticelli e il ricamo del Museo Poldi Pezzoli: Storia di un restauro*, Milan c.1990, pp. 87–93; L. Masschelein-Kleiner and L. Maes, 'Etude technique de la tapisserie tournaisienne aux XV\u1D49 et XVI\u1D49 siècles. Les colorants', *Bulletin de l'Institut Royal du Patrimoine Artistique*, XII, 1970, pp. 269–79; 'Etude technique de la tapisserie des Pays-Bas méridionaux. Les tapisseries anversoises des XVI\u1D49 et XVII\u1D49 siècles. Les teintures', *Bulletin de l'Institut Royal du Patrimoine Artistique*, XVI, 1976/77, pp. 143–53; J. Wouters, 'Analyse des colorants des tapisseries brugeoises des XVI\u1D49 et XVII\u1D49 siècles' in G. Delmarcel and E. Duverger, *Bruges et la tapisserie*, Bruges 1987, pp. 515–26. It is worth noting that Southern Europe, notably Italy, was for many years the source of fine silks, while the wool industry was at the same time of similar importance in Northern Europe.

46. Brunello, 1968, cited in note 3, pp. 143–4; Francesco Balducci Pegolotti, [*Libro di divisamenti di paesi e di misuri di mercatanzie e d'altre cose bisogneroli di sapere a' mercatanti*, c. 1339–40] *La pratica della mercatura*, edited by A. Evans, Cambridge, Mass. 1936, p. 371; A. Nannizzi, *L'Arte degli Speziali in Siena*, Siena 1939, p. 43. Madder was cultivated in Lombardy and other parts of Italy. It should be remembered that leather was also dyed, using the same dyestuffs; brazilwood and madder are mentioned in this context: see, for example, *Segreti per colori*; the Bolognese manuscript (Bologna, Biblioteca dell'Università, MS 2681, fifteenth century) in M.P. Merrifield, *Original Treatises dating from the XIIth to the XVIIIth centuries on*

the Arts of Painting, London 1849 (Dover reprint, New York and London 1967), Vol. II, no. 110, pp. 546–57.

47. Masschelein-Kleiner and Maes, 1976/77, cited in note 45; G. Rosetti, [*Plictho de larte de tentori*] *The Plictho of Gioanventura Rosetti*, trs. S.M. Edelstein and H.C. Borghetty, Cambridge, Mass. and London 1969 (includes facsimile of 1st edn., Venice 1548), pp. 18, 107–8 (for example).

48. L. Guicciardini, *Descrittione di M. Lodovico Guicciardini patritio fiorentino, di tutti i paesi bassi, altrimenti detti Germania inferiore*, Antwerp 1567, pp. 60–115, 119–20; *Tarifa zoè noticia dy pexi e mexure di luoghi e tere che s'adovra marcadantia per el mondo*, [later fourteenth or early fifteenth century], R. Istituto Superiore di Scienze Economiche e Commerciale de Venezia, Venice 1925; L. Lazzarini, 'Il colore nei pittori veneziani tra il 1480 e il 1580', *Bollettino d'Arte*, supplement 5, 1983, pp. 135–44, especially pp. 135–6.

49. Sanyova and Wouters, 1993, cited in note 24, pp. 39–41.

50. J. Decaisne, 'Recherches anatomiques et physiologiques sur la garance', *Mémoires couronnés par l'Académie Royale des Sciences et Belle-lettres de Bruxelles*, 12, 1837 (2nd essay); see plate 6. The authors are grateful to Dr David Hill, Department for Continuing Education, University of Bristol, for bringing this reference to their attention.

51. P. Miller, *The Method of Cultivating Madder, as it is now practised by the Dutch in Zealand ...*, London 1758, pp. 10–11; C. Wiskerke, 'De geschiedenis van het meekrapbedrijf in Nederland', *Economisch-Historisch Jaarboek*, XXV, 1952, pp. 1–144; see pp. 44–9, especially Plate V.

52. G.A. Fokker, 'De oudst bekende keur op het bereiden van en den handel in meekrap in Zeeland', *Archief Vroegere en Latere Mededeelingen Voornamelijk in Betrekking tot Zeeland*, II, 1866–69, vi, pp. 317–28. The authors are grateful to Dr Lorne Campbell for this reference.

53. Wiskerke, 1952, cited in note 51; G. Asaert, 'Handel in kleurstoffen op de Antwerpse markt tijdens de XVe eeuw', *Bijdragen en Mededelingen betreffende de geschiedenis der Nederlanden*, 88, 3, 1973, pp. 377–402.

54. P.J. Garidel, *Histoire des plantes qui naissent aux environs d'Aix et des plusieurs autres endroits de la Provence*, Aix 1715, pp. 247–55; plate 53 (following p. 260).

55. Wouters and Verhecken, 1991, cited in note 22, pp. 219–20; Sanyova and Wouters, 1993, cited in note 24, pp. 40–1.

56. Pegolotti/Evans, 1936, cited in note 46, p. 297; G. Gargiolli, *L'Arte della seta in Firenze; trattato del secolo XV*, Florence 1868, p. 109; varieties of *chermisi* are also listed. Several fifteenth and sixteenth-century manuscripts of the treatise exist; the most complete version is one in the Biblioteca Riccardiana, Florence, MS 2580. Gargiolli thought all were copies of a lost original dating from the end of the fourteenth or early fifteenth century. See also A. Doren, *Studien aus der Florentiner Wirtschaftsgeschichte*, Vol. 1: *Die florentiner Wollentuchindustrie vom vierzehnten bis zum sechszehnten Jahrhundert*, Stuttgart 1901, pp. 484–93

57. Rosetti, 1548 (1969 reprint), cited in note 47: *grana*, pp. 5–6, 94; 45, 136; *cremesino*, pp. 47, 138–9.

58. Gargiolli, 1868, cited in note 56, p. 78.

59. Verhecken and Wouters, 1988/89, cited in note 3, pp. 226–9.

60. Pegolotti/Evans, 1936, cited in note 46, pp. 361, 366, 371, 382–3. Similar, less detailed, descriptions are found in later merchants' handbooks.

61. [The *Nürnberger Kunstbuch*, Nürnberger Stadtbibliothek, MS cent. VI, 89, mid-fifteenth century] E.E. Ploss, *Ein Buch von alten Farben: Technologie der Textilfarben im Mittelalter mit einem Ausblick auf die festen Farben*, Heidelberg and Berlin 1962, p. 113; *Middelnederlandse verfrecepten voor miniaturen en 'alderhande substancien'*, ed. W.L. Braekman, Brussels 1986 (SCRIPTA Mediaeval and Renaissance Texts and Studies, Vol. 18, published by the Research Center of Mediaeval and Renaissance Studies, Brussels): Text I (MS 517, Wellcome Historical Medical Library, London, late fifteenth century, extracts), no. 45, pp. 46–7 ; Text II, (*T'Bouck van Wondre*, Brussels 1513), no. 9 (on dyeing '*vlocken*'), p. 66; *Instruction générale pour la teinture des laines*, Paris 1671, pp. 24–5, 31, 73.

62. Braekman, 1986, ibid., Text I, no. 45, pp. 46–7; Ploss, 1962, ibid., pp. 113–14.

63. P. de La Hyre, 'Traité de la pratique de peinture', *Mémoires de l'Académie Royale des Sciences depuis 1666 jusqu'à 1699*, IX, Paris 1730, pp. 637–730; see p. 670. (Published posthumously; based on a lecture given to the Académie in 1709.)

64. *Segreti per colori* [the Bolognese manuscript], Merrifield Vol. II, 1849, cited in note 46, no. 110, pp. 432–5. In other recipes (B.139, pp. 456–7) it appears that the alkali was stronger and that the fibres dissolved to a large extent. See also Wallert, 1991, cited in note 5, p. 82, note 5.

65. U. Birkmaier, A. Wallert and A. Rothe, 'Technical Examination of Titian's *Venus and Adonis*: A Note on Early Italian Oil Painting Technique', *Historical Painting Techniques, Materials and Studio Practice: Preprints of a Symposium, University of Leiden, the Netherlands, 26-29 June 1995*, edited by

A. Wallert, E. Hermens and M. Peek, Malibu 1995, pp. 117–26, especially p. 123.

66. J. Murrell, 'John Guillim's Book: A Heraldic Painter's *Vade Mecum*', *The Walpole Society*, LVII, 1993/94, pp. 1–51, especially p. 25: 'To Make a Red Rose'. (National Art Library MS L. 1774-1935, press mark 86. EE. 69.)

67. J. Plesters and L. Lazzarini, 'I materiali e la tecnica del Tintoretto della Scuola di San Rocco', *Atti di Convegno Internazionale di Studi su Jacopo Tintoretto nel IV centennario della morte, Venice 1994*, in press.

68. Kirby, 1977, cited in note 4, pp. 40, 42; C. Brown and A. Roy, 'Rembrandt's "Alexander the Great"', *Burlington Magazine*, CXXXIV, no. 1070, 1992, pp. 286–97, especially pp. 291, 293–4.

69. J.H. Hofenk de Graaff, '"Woven Bouquet": Dyestuff-Analysis on a Group of Northern Dutch flowered Table-cloths and Tapestries of the 17th Century', *ICOM Committee for Conservation, 4th Triennial Meeting, Venice, 13-18 October, 1975: Preprints*, Venice 1975, pp. 75/10/3/1–15; [D.W.S.d.H.n., *Dat oprecht secret van dat roet scherlaeken met sijn apendicht ...*, 1631] N.W. Posthumus and W.L.J. de Nie, 'Een Handschrift over de textielververij in de Republiek uit de eerste helft der zeventiende eeuw', *Nederlandsch Economisch-Historisch Archief Jaarboek*, XX, 1936, pp. 212–57, especially pp. 234–7, 244. Posthumus identifies the author of the manuscript, which is in the Economisch-Historisch Bibliotheek, Amsterdam, as Dirc Willemsz. van der Heyden.

70. F. Pritchard, 'Dyes on some 16th- and 17th-century textiles excavated in London', *Dyes in History and Archaeology*, 10, 1991, pp. 38–41

71. For an account of this analysis see Claire Chorley, *The Cleaning and Restoration of William Larkin's Portrait of Susan Villiers, Countess of Denbigh*, unpublished essay for the Conservation of Easel Paintings course, Hamilton Kerr Institute, University of Cambridge. Thanks are due to Ian McClure and Renate Woudhuysen Keller for permission to publish this result.

72. Sanyova and Wouters, 1993, cited in note 24, pp. 39–41.

73. See, for example, Rosetti, 1548 (1969 reprint), cited in note 47, pp. 20, 110; 28, 118; 36, 127–8; 62–3, 155–6

74. See, for example, Rosetti, ibid., pp. 23–4, 114; 28, 118; *Instruction générale pour la teinture des laines*, cited in note 61, p. 24.

75. Gargiolli, 1868, cited in note 56, pp. 33, 56, 69, 134; Rosetti, ibid., pp. 44–6, 134–7; 50–51, 142–3; 53–4, 145–7; Verhecken and Wouters, 1988/89, cited in note 3, pp. 215–16, 227.

76. Pegolotti/Evans, 1936, cited in note 46, p. 366;

Cardon, *Les 'vers' du rouge*, 1990, cited in note 3, pp. 110–12.

77. Garcia da Orta, *Colloquies on the Simples and Drugs of India*, edited and annotated by the Conde de Ficalho, translated by Sir Clements Markham, London 1913, pp. 240–50 (first edn. Goa 1563).

78. E. Bancroft, *Experimental Researches concerning the Philosophy of Permanent Colours...*, 2 vols., London 1813, Vol. II, pp. 1–59.

79. La Hyre, 1730, cited in note 63, pp. 670–2; H. Gautier, *L'Art de laver, ou Nouvelle manière de peindre sur le papier*, Lyon 1687 (facsimile reprint Portland, Oreg. 1972), pp. 49–52. With the chromatographic system described, no distinction between cochineal carmine and cochineal lake can be made.

80. J. Dunkerton and A. Roy, 'The Materials of a Group of late Fifteenth-century Florentine Panel Paintings', in this *Bulletin*, pp. 20–31, especially p. 28; J. Dunkerton, 'The Painting Technique of the Manchester Madonna' in M. Hirst and J. Dunkerton, *Making and Meaning: The Young Michelangelo*, exhibition catalogue, London 1994, pp. 83–105. In the case of the Michelangelo painting, the presence of a trace of kermes lake was suspected, but could not be confirmed.

81. P. Bensi, 'Gli Gesuati dell'arte. I Gesuati di San Giusto alle Mura e la pittura del rinascimento a Firenze', *Studi di Storia delle Arti*, 1980, pp. 33–47, especially p. 41.

82. Neri di Bicci, *Le ricordanze (10 marzo 1453 – 24 aprile 1475)*, edited by Bruno Santi, Pisa 1976, pp. 270, 279, 316–18, 328, 366. The Florentine ounce was equivalent to *c.*28.3g; there were 12 ounces to the pound in Italy: see Bomford et al., 1989, cited in note 43, pp. 205–6.

83. Lorenzo Lotto, *Il 'Libro di spese diverse' con aggiunta di lettere e d'altri documenti*, edited by P. Zampetti, Venice and Rome 1969, p. 238; an even more expensive lake, from the Bolognese architect Sebastiano Serlio, is mentioned on p. 234. The portrait may be that referred to on p. 98.

84. Wallert, 1991, cited in note 5, pp. 79–81.

85. J. Hellot, *L'art de la teinture des laines et les étoffes de laine en grand et petit teint*, Paris 1750, pp. 244–5; R. Blanchard, *Les coccidés utiles: Thèse présentée au concours d'agrégation (Anatomie, Physiologie et histoire naturelle), Faculté de Médecine de Paris*, Meulan 1883, pp. 56–7; W. Born, 'Scarlet', *Ciba Review*, 7, 1938, pp. 206–27, especially pp. 212–14.

86. Blanchard, ibid., pp. 58–60.

87. Chr.H. Schmidt, *Vollständiges Farben-Laboratorium*, 2nd edn., Weimar 1847 (1st edn. 1841), pp. 454–6; G. Field, *Examples and Anecdotes of Pigments. Practical Journal 1809*, f. 332. Field Manuscripts, Field/6, photographic copy, Courtauld Institute Library, London.

88. L. Keith and A. Roy, 'Giampietrino, Boltraffio and the Influence of Leonardo', in this *Bulletin*, pp. 4–19, especially note 39, p. 19.

89. Red glaze on the Virgin's robe in *The Coronation of the Virgin* (NG 1897), the central panel of the altarpiece of which NG 216 forms a part, was thought to contain lac lake, but it could be examined by microspectrophotometry only; see A. Burnstock, 'The Fading of the Virgin's Robe in Lorenzo Monaco's "Coronation of the Virgin"', *National Gallery Technical Bulletin*, 12, 1988, pp. 58–65.

90. Examination by TLC suggested that lac lake had been used; it must be assumed that the kermes dyestuff present had been altered beyond recognition by the boron trifluoride reagent as described in the text. The glaze, in an egg tempera medium, is painted over silver leaf; both silver and glaze have deteriorated, but the chemical effect on the dyestuff has not been elucidated: see D. Bomford and J. Kirby, 'Giovanni di Paolo's "SS. Fabian and Sebastian"', *National Gallery Technical Bulletin*, 2, 1978, pp. 56–65 and Plate 8, pp. 46–7, especially pp. 64–5 and Plate 8a.

91. This confirms the result obtained by TLC in 1977.

92. Penny and Spring, 1995, cited in note 42, p. 15 and note 51, p. 27.

93. For a discussion of Veronese's *Allegories* and *The Adoration of the Kings*, see N. Penny, A. Roy and M. Spring, 'Veronese's Paintings in the National Gallery. Technique and Materials: Part II', in this *Bulletin*, pp. 32–55, especially p. 49.

94. Lac lake was identified in samples from Jupiter's cloak and the drapery over the bed by TLC: see J. Plesters, 'Tintoretto's Paintings in the National Gallery', *National Gallery Technical Bulletin*, 4, 1980, pp. 32–47, especially p. 39 (compare results from NG 1130, *Christ washing his Disciples' Feet*, p. 37).

95. This painting was formerly ascribed to Murillo.

96. It seems likely that the work now visible has been painted over an earlier, seventeenth-century composition, perhaps a version of the same subject: see M. Levey, *National Gallery Catalogues: 17th and 18th Century Italian Schools*, London 1971, p. 192. The sample examined was from the lower, seventeenth-century, paint. Carminic acid was found to be present, but the insect source could not be determined because of interference from other organic components.

97. The presence of madder dyestuff in addition to that extracted from kermes could not be confirmed.

98. Madder alone appeared to be present in a sample taken from the red paint of the carpet in the companion panel, *The Mass of Saint Giles* (NG 4681), examined by microspectrophotometry and TLC; see D. Bomford and J. Kirby, 'Two Panels by the Master of Saint Giles', *National Gallery Technical Bulletin*, 1, 1977, pp. 46–56, especially p. 55.

99. The chromatogram also revealed the presence of alizarin crimson retouching.

100. The presence of kermes dyestuff in addition to the madder could not be confirmed.

101. This result may appear unusual in a Northern European context; the picture was painted in London, however, and there are no analytical results from English paintings of this period for comparison.

102. R. White and J. Kirby, 'Rembrandt and his Circle: Seventeenth-Century Dutch Paint Media Re-examined', *National Gallery Technical Bulletin*, 15, 1994, pp. 64–78, especially p. 73, Plate 2, p. 66 and note 60, p. 77.

103. The sample was extremely small and contained much drying oil, obscuring the chromatogram to such an extent that it is not possible to rule out the presence of lac lake; cochineal lake was identified in Rubens's *Elevation of the Cross*; see Wouters, 1992, cited in note 24, p. 82.

104. J. Pilc and R. White, 'The Application of FTIR-Microscopy to the Analysis of Paint Binders in Easel Paintings', *National Gallery Technical Bulletin*, 16, 1995, pp. 73–84, especially pp. 82–3 and Fig. 8, p. 79.

105. J. Kirby and A. Roy, 'Paul Delaroche: A Case Study of Academic Painting', *Historical Painting Techniques, Materials and Studio Practice*, 1995, cited in note 65, pp. 166–75, especially p. 172.

106. Saunders and Kirby, 1994, cited in note 4, pp. 79–97, especially pp. 79–80.

107. Cochineal lake was also identified in the sitter's coat in Gainsborough's *Dr Ralph Schomberg* (NG 684); see D. Bomford, A. Roy and D. Saunders, 'Gainsborough's "Dr Ralph Schomberg"', *National Gallery Technical Bulletin*, 12, 1988, pp. 44–57, especially pp. 51–4.

Long-term Colour Change Measurement: Some Results after Twenty Years

DAVID SAUNDERS, HELENE CHAHINE AND JOHN CUPITT

Some twenty years ago, after a period of research and development,[1] the Scientific Department at the National Gallery began to make accurate colour measurements on a number of paintings in the Collection, with a view to detecting and measuring any subsequent changes.[2] Ten years later, an analysis of the results obtained using the Wright-Wassall reflectance spectrophotometer detected changes at the surface of the painting due to the slight yellowing or matting of the varnish layer, but found no indication of colour changes in the pigments resulting from long-term display in the galleries.[3]

Unfortunately, it became clear some years ago that certain components in the spectrophotometer, particularly the fibre-optic link from the monochromator to the measuring head, were gradually deteriorating, causing considerable differences in the colour measurements. Although these parts could be replaced, the reproducibility of colour measurement could not be ensured. When it was clear that the colour measurements being made were no longer comparable to those recorded some years earlier, the long-term monitoring of paintings using the spectrophotometer ceased.

By this time, the programme of direct colour measurement from paintings by means of electronic imaging, first developed in the early 1980s,[4] had reached a stage where digital images of paintings that afforded accurate colorimetric information were being made. In the long term, direct comparison of images made at, for example, five-yearly intervals will be used to assess and quantify changes in appearance. Although the electronic imaging system has been used to measure colour in paintings before, during and after conservation treatment,[5] no painting has yet been remeasured after a period of 'normal' display in the Gallery.

While waiting for sufficient time to elapse to make meaningful comparisons between colorimetric images of paintings, we were anxious to make use of the measurements made in the 1970s and 1980s using the Wright-Wassall spectrophotometer. This is particularly important as the few studies of colour changes in works of art under display conditions either covered relatively short periods[6] or are still in their early stages.[7] Accordingly, we have set out to compare colour measurements made with the spectrophotometer with those being made with the electronic imaging system, and in so doing, to assess the degree of colour change that has occurred over a period of up to twenty years.

Comparing the colour data from the two techniques

The colour data from the Wright-Wassall spectrophotometer are expressed in the form of CIE L*, a* and b* values for a number of areas on the surface of each painting studied.[8] The instrument measured spectral reflectance from a roughly circular area of diameter c. 4mm. As previously described,[9] the colour data are accompanied by a photographic record of the position of each measurement. This record was intended to allow the spectrophotometer to be repositioned precisely during subsequent remeasurement. These photographs, a series of black and white 35mm negatives, have allowed us to locate accurately the area of each original reflectance measurement so that the corresponding data can be extracted from the high-resolution colour image of the painting. The procedure for comparison is described below and illustrated in Plate 1, using as an example one area from *The Adoration of the Kings* by the Master of Liesborn (NG 258), illustrated in

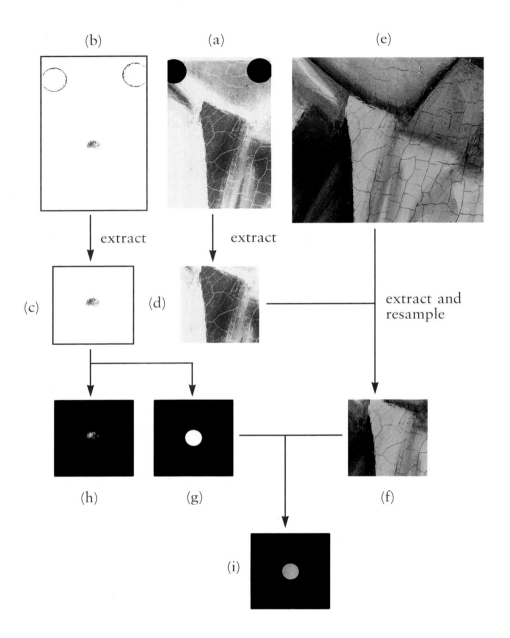

Plate 1 Schematic representation of the procedure for determining CIE data from the colorimetric image:

(a) digitised image of the 35mm negative made during the spectrophotometric measurement of the green area of *The Adoration of the Kings* (NG 258) marked as point 2 in Plate 2

(b) digitised image of the 35mm negative showing the 'spot' covered by the spectrophotometer during colour measurement of *The Adoration of the Kings*

(c) region extracted from image b

(d) corresponding region extracted from image a

(e) sub-image extracted from the region of the high-resolution digitised image of *The Adoration of the Kings* centred on point 2 in Plate 2

(f) region of image e after extraction and resampling so as to coincide exactly with image d

(g) circular mask created with the same centre and diameter as the spot in image c; white represents a numerical value of one, and black a value of zero

(h) mask created by scaling the lightness values of the spot in image d to fall within the range zero to one; white and black again represent one and zero respectively, while intermediate values appear as shades of grey

(i) image created by combining the circular mask represented by image g with the resampled colour image, image f

Plate 2. The sample area chosen is on the sleeve of the green robe of the right-hand figure, marked on Plate 2 as point 2.

Analysing the photographic record

The first step in the comparison process is to digitise the 35mm negatives that record the measurement sites for the spectrophotometer using a commercial slide- or desktop-scanner. Plate 1a shows the digitised image of the negative made during the spectrophotometric measurement of point 2. The optics of the spectrophotometer were designed so that, theoretically, the 4mm diameter measurement area 'spot' would be at the centre of the negative. It is clear, however, that slight variations in position exist. To determine the exact position of the spot, we were fortunate to have additional 35mm negatives, made at the time of each measurement, that show the position and shape of the spot. These were also digitised, Plate 1b, and used to identify the exact area on which the original measurement was made. A square region is extracted from the image of the spot. This image is chosen so that its centre corresponds to the centre of the spot, Plate 1c. From the image of the measurement area (Plate 1a) an identical region is extracted, Plate 1d.

Analysing the colorimetric image

The colour images that provide information on the current colour of the painting are acquired using the VASARI image processing system described in an earlier paper.[10] Recent improvements in the equipment and calibration procedures have increased the colour accuracy of the images used in this study.[11] First, an area on the colour image roughly corresponding to that covered by the 35mm negative is extracted from the image of the whole painting, Plate 1e. By selecting 'tie points' that appear on both this image and on the region extracted from the monochrome image (Plate 1d), the former is resampled to coincide exactly with the latter.[12] The resampled colour image is shown in Plate 1f.

The next step is to extract from the resampled colour image that region which corresponds to the area of the spot measured by the spectrophotometer. Two methods of extraction

were investigated. In the first, a circular 'mask' is created, which has the same centre and diameter as the spot illustrated in Plate 1c. All the pixels within the circle have a value of one, while all those in the surrounding region are set at zero. This first mask is represented in Plate 1g (zero is represented as black and one as white). In the second method, the value of each pixel within the circular mask was determined by scaling the image of the spot to fit in the range zero to one. Plate 1h illustrates the second mask, which represents more accurately the distribution of the incident illumination during the original spectrophotometric measurement.

By combining the chosen mask with the extracted, resampled, colorimetric image and then averaging the CIE L*, a* and b* values within that region, it is possible to calculate the current CIE L*, a* and b* coordinates for the area studied previously with the spectrophotometer;[13] the result of combining the circular mask (Plate 1g) with the resampled colour image (Plate 1f) is shown in Plate 1i. Finally, the colour difference between the two measurements (spectrophotometer and imaging system) is calculated and expressed in the CIE units of colour difference, ΔE.[14]

A series of tests was conducted to assess the effect on the average colorimetric data of using the two types of mask described above to extract the information from the resampled colorimetric image. It was found that using a mask that simulated the exact shape of the spot measured by the spectrophotometer, shown in Plate 1h, produced results that were virtually indistinguishable from those produced using a mask in which the spot was simulated by a perfect circle, shown in Plate 1g.[15] Since the latter is more easily generated, we used a simple circular mask in all subsequent studies.

Results and discussion

During 1994 and 1995 a number of the paintings that had been measured with the spectrophotometer have been imaged colorimetrically with the VASARI system and the current colour compared with the Scientific Department's record of colour measurements in the 1970s and 1980s using the procedure outlined above.

Plate 2 The Master of Liesborn, *The Adoration of the Kings* (NG 258). The areas on which colour measurements were made are indicated; the numbering corresponds to entries in Table 1.

Table 1 Colour and colour change data for the Master of Liesborn, *The Adoration of the Kings*

Point number and colour description	CIE Colour coordinates (1994)			Colour change from 1984 to 1994			
	L*	a*	b*	ΔL*	Δa*	Δb*	ΔE
1. White	69.59	1.00	6.92	0.56	0.90	0.03	1.06
2. Pale green	58.38	−10.05	23.58	1.25	1.37	−1.19	2.20
3. Pink	45.60	20.91	5.60	1.13	−0.41	1.12	1.64
4. Crimson	7.78	34.59	8.42	−10.09	10.83	−1.44	14.87
5. Crimson	10.31	22.97	10.66	−6.98	5.82	2.89	9.53
6. Red	33.50	36.95	38.51	−1.24	4.70	9.72	10.87
7. Yellow	63.21	1.17	23.62	−0.53	−1.68	−3.09	3.56
8. Green	35.00	−16.73	21.60	−1.49	−0.94	2.91	3.40
9. Dark blue	6.63	−7.31	0.80	−7.85	−3.85	2.63	9.13
10. Blue	30.22	−9.36	−13.47	−1.14	−0.57	−0.43	1.35
11. Flesh	52.61	9.00	11.41	−0.17	1.21	0.23	1.25
12. Gold	61.49	7.06	43.45	−0.60	1.72	1.16	2.16
13. Red	34.06	7.02	6.75	−0.84	0.17	0.93	1.27
14. Green	41.14	−18.06	18.67	−3.00	−0.90	−1.38	3.42
15. Pale blue	55.91	−3.87	−3.40	−0.19	−0.33	−0.01	0.38

Colour difference data for the three paintings in which significant colour changes were detected are given in Tables 1 to 3. As the electronic imaging system has an accuracy of approximately 1.5–2.0ΔE units,[16] we have assumed, in the discussion below, that colour changes of less than 4.0ΔE units (twice the maximum error) are not significant, although we believe that some changes below this threshold are not attributable to experimental error. The majority of the areas studied showed colour differences of less than 4.0ΔE units, and often less than 2.0ΔE units, indicating no measurable colour change. For each painting for which data are tabulated there were, however, significant changes in one or more of the areas investigated, which we have attempted to describe and explain in the sections that follow.

The Master of Liesborn: *The Adoration of the Kings*

This painting is illustrated in Plate 2, which shows the areas at which colour measurements were made; the colour and colour change data are presented in Table 1. Only four of the fifteen areas studied show significant colour differences. Of these four, three (two areas of crimson and one of dark blue) have very low lightness, with an L* of *c*.10 or less. Several possible sources of error were investigated to determine whether this was purely coincidental. Colour change in only the dark areas suggested that perhaps the less rigid geometry of illumination used in the imaging system might cause some specular reflection to enter the camera. In the spectrophotometer, the angle of illumination is exactly 45° to the surface of the painting, while the lighting system in the imaging system is only approximately at this angle. The changes observed are not, however, consistent with such an effect. If specular reflection were present, an increase in lightness and a decrease in saturation (colourfulness) would be expected. It is clear that in this painting the colour change is characterised by decreased lightness and increased saturation. We believe that the reason for the colour differences for the very dark areas in this painting is light scatter within the camera optics. The calibration procedure for colorimetric imaging optimises the system for imaging a calibration target com-prising the 24 patches of the Macbeth ColorChecker Chart, which have an average L* of 47.59. If there are particularly dark regions, as in this painting, there will be less scatter and the colours will appear darker and more saturated. At present we are attempting to model better the scattering effect so that we can compensate for this problem, which can afflict all imaging systems, electronic or conventional.

The fourth area, the red sleeve of the figure to the left (point 6), is much lighter and thus unlikely to be affected by the light scatter problem. This is borne out by the observation that the colour difference is largely due to changes in a* and b*. The main colour change in this area is an increase in b*, or an increased yellowness. No such change in b* is exhibited by any of the other areas of measurement suggesting that this is a localised yellowing and not an overall yellowing of the varnish. Why only this robe, which seems to be painted using vermilion with a red lake glaze in the shadows[17], should have yellowed is not clear.

The remaining eleven areas investigated show small colour differences, indicating that there are no other colour changes occurring in the painting. The absence of colour change in the pink collar of the king at the right is particularly interesting, as it seems likely that the same lake pigment that occurs in the two deep crimson areas (points 4 and 5) has also been used here, mixed with white.[18] Although the results for the two darker areas are inconclusive, due to the problems with colour measurement in the darker areas described above, it seems reasonable to conclude that these will not have not changed either, since it is known that mixtures with white are more prone to colour change than the pure lake.[19]

Corot: *The Roman Campagna, with the Claudian Aqueduct*

This painting is illustrated in Plate 3, which shows the areas at which colour measurements were made; the colour and colour change data are presented in Table 2. Some colour change was observed in the two green areas monitored and a smaller change in the dark purple area on the horizon, Plate 3. The two green areas show sizeable changes in b*, but in one case an increase and in the other a decrease. The two

Plate 3 Jean-Baptiste-Camille Corot, *The Roman Campagna, with the Claudian Aqueduct* (NG 3285). The areas on which colour measurements were made are indicated; the numbering corresponds to entries in Table 2.

Table 2 Colour and colour change data for Corot, *The Roman Campagna, with the Claudian Aqueduct*

Point number and colour description	CIE Colour coordinates (1995)			Colour change from 1982 to 1995			
	L^*	a^*	b^*	ΔL^*	Δa^*	Δb^*	ΔE
1. White	70.69	3.01	20.77	2.78	0.33	0.52	2.85
2. Turquoise	60.71	−4.05	11.87	1.09	0.58	0.03	1.23
3. Blue sky	51.13	−4.06	−4.89	1.09	1.54	−0.46	1.94
4. Dark purple	29.94	2.64	−5.47	−4.05	2.39	−1.00	4.81
5. Light purple	54.84	2.13	1.30	−0.57	1.64	0.84	1.87
6. Green	45.57	−3.56	14.45	2.17	0.00	−8.02	8.31
7. Green	28.12	−0.19	31.66	−5.82	0.23	11.34	12.75

areas are quite different and illustrate two of the problems which can arise when determining the exact position of the mask on the colour image.

First, some regions on each painting contain few distinctive features by which to make the image comparison between the extracts from the high-resolution image and the monochrome image of the 35mm negative. In such cases, including the uniform streak of green paint on which point 6 lies, it is difficult to determine the exact position of the spot. Fortunately, as these areas tend to be homogeneous, the need to locate the mask with high accuracy is less, and we have found that displacement of the spot by around 20% of its diameter produces little change in the average L^*, a^* and b^* values.[20]

The second area (point 7), in a bush to the right of the painting is, like many areas studied, very inhomogeneous in colour. We therefore investigated the effect of displacing the mask from its calculated position by up to 20% of its diameter. None of the colour measurements for this painting, including those for point 7, showed any significant colour change when the spot was moved away from its calculated position.[21] Where small colour changes have been observed on shifting the mask, L* was most affected with only small changes to a* and b*; that is, the lightness changed but the hue remained invariant.

Because of its small size we were able to examine the surface of the painting under the optical microscope at high magnification.[22] The purple paint comprises vermilion and cobalt blue, with some carbon black in the darker areas. It is conceivable that the colour change in this region has occurred because the vermilion component has darkened, but in view of the increase in redness (increase in a*), this seems unlikely. We were concerned that this change might be due to another potential source of error in the calibration procedure. The figure quoted earlier for colour accuracy, 1.5 to 2.0ΔE units, is an average for the 24 patches in the Macbeth chart used in the calibration procedure. We were also concerned that although the average might be as low as 1.5ΔE units, the greatest colour difference for one individual patch might be considerably higher, implying that the colour accuracy of the image was poor for certain colours. We have therefore compared the colour difference data for each area that we believe has changed with the colour difference data for the Macbeth patch closest in colour to the area under investigation. In this painting the highest colour error for any of the individual patches was 2.6ΔE units, and the error for the purple Macbeth patch (closest in colour to the area under study) was only 0.9ΔE units.

Examination under the microscope revealed that the green paint comprises a stable inorganic green with varying amounts of a yellow earth pigment and carbon black. The mixture also contains some large translucent dull-yellow particles that may be a yellow lake pigment or another organic yellow. If such a lake pigment faded in the mixture, an increase in lightness and a decrease in yellowness might be expected, exactly as observed for the pale green streak at point 6.

Uccello: *Saint George and the Dragon*

This painting is illustrated in Plate 4, which also shows the areas at which colour measurements were made; the colour and colour change data are presented in Table 3. *Saint George and the Dragon* was one of the first paintings to be recorded by the colour measurement programme in 1974. Much interest centred on the area of grass at the lower edge that had been protected from light in the past by a frame rebate. As the painting has subsequently been framed in such a way as to expose this area to light, it is of concern to discover whether the then relatively unchanged area of 'copper resinate' at point 1 has now changed. The data in Table 3 indicate that this is one of the few areas of this painting where any significant change has occurred: there has been a slight decrease in lightness and a more marked increase in yellowness. Because this area of the painting depicts blades of grass, it is particularly inhomogeneous in colour. The position of the mask is, therefore, very important if a meaningful comparison is to be made. Displacing the mask, as described previously, results in little change in the value of Δb*, but has rather more effect on the value of ΔL* which can be as much as −2.98. The changes of colour observed are consistent with a shift from green towards brown in this region, but it remains for the future to see if this trend will continue.

Conclusions

In spite of the considerable differences between the two techniques for colour measurement, it has been possible to make meaningful comparisons between the colour data recorded up to twenty years ago using the spectrophotometer, and those being made today with the electronic imaging system. This is particularly important since there would be no way to replace the early data.

Several sources for potential error in the comparison process have been investigated and all except the problem associated with the measurement of very dark colours have been overcome satisfactorily. An improved calibration procedure, which compensates for light scatter when measuring dark colours, is being explored. As it is usually the lighter colours that

Plate 4   Paolo Uccello, *Saint George and the Dragon* (NG 6294). The areas on which colour measurements were made are indicated; the numbering corresponds to entries in Table 3.

Table 3 Colour and colour change data for Uccello, *Saint George and the Dragon*

Point number and colour description	CIE Colour coordinates (1995)			Colour change from 1974 to 1995			
	L*	a*	b*	ΔL*	Δa*	Δb*	ΔE
1. Green	24.27	−3.76	18.06	−0.70	1.02	8.34	8.43
2. Brown	14.94	0.24	7.49	−3.65	0.10	2.51	4.43
3. Blue †	26.78	−8.49	−3.78	3.98	−2.40	−2.77	5.41
4. Pale blue †	43.10	−6.94	1.37	3.15	−1.22	1.13	3.56
5. Blue †	23.90	−9.62	1.13	0.21	−1.53	−0.25	1.56
6. Dark pink †	26.67	17.36	5.61	3.17	1.41	−1.28	3.70
7. Pale pink †	46.10	9.14	7.48	4.15	1.45	1.00	4.51
8. Red †	30.97	5.70	6.81	2.50	1.00	−0.89	2.83
9. Red †	32.06	25.51	23.58	0.87	3.29	4.36	5.53
10. White †	45.35	0.89	10.74	3.43	0.58	1.25	3.70
11. Green †	20.62	−4.27	17.71	−1.80	6.09	5.03	8.10
12. Beige †	38.75	5.91	5.30	3.30	2.81	0.13	4.34

† Area first measured in 1980. Colour change is for the period 1980 to 1995.

are most prone to colour change,[23] the lack of data for the dark regions of some paintings is not too serious.

In the majority of the paintings studied, no significant colour changes have been detected. In a few cases, some of the areas examined have shown differences in colour that might be explained by the presence of pigments known to be susceptible to colour change over time. In a final, very small group, are changes that cannot easily be attributed to known pigment alteration processes but which do not seem to be purely the result of experimental error.

A particular difficulty in trying to make comparisons with the data from the spectrophotometer is that each colour measurement corresponds to a single point. It is not possible to assess whether a change noted in one 4mm diameter region within a larger area of a single colour is a 'rogue' result, or reflects a change throughout the area painted with that pigment. When, in the future, colorimetric images of the painting are compared, this problem should be minimised as the area of paint will be covered by many thousands, or tens of thousands, of pixels, each of which will provide colour information.

The present study has provided information to bridge the old and new regimes for long-term colour measurement. The images we are recording now will provide our successors with a colour record with which to make comparisons in twenty years time, and meanwhile maintain continuity with the original spectrophotometric measurements made twenty years ago.

Acknowledgements
We are grateful to Ashok Roy, Marika Spring, Jo Kirby and Rachel Billinge for their observations on, and identification of the pigments in, Corot's *The Roman Campagna, with the Claudian Aqueduct* and *The Adoration of the Kings* by the Master of Liesborn. We would also like to thank Kirk Martinez of Birkbeck College, University of London, for his expertise, and assistance in digitising the 35mm negatives. The imaging systems and software described in this paper were developed in the European Community-funded ESPRIT projects VASARI (No. 2649) and MARC (No. 6937). Hélène Chahine, from the Ecole Nationale Supérieure

Physique de Strasbourg, was a researcher in the Scientific Department during 1994–5.

Notes and references
1. M.P. Wassall and W.D. Wright, 'A special-purpose spectrophotometer', *Colour 73*, London 1973, pp. 469–71; G. Thomson, 'Current Researches on Colour Change in Paintings at the National Gallery, London', *Preprints of the International Council of Museums Committee for Conservation*, 4th triennial meeting, Venice 1975, 75/19/1.
2. The long-term monitoring of paintings using the Wright-Wassall spectrophotometer was first reported in L. Bullock, 'Reflectance Spectrophotometry for Measurement of Colour Change', *National Gallery Technical Bulletin*, 2 , 1978, pp. 49–55.
3. D. Saunders, 'The Measurement of Colour Change in Paintings', *European Spectroscopy News*, 67, 1986, pp. 10–18.
4. The stages of development of the programme of long-term monitoring of paintings by image processing are described in G. Thomson and S. Staniforth, 'Identification and Measurement of Change in Appearance by Image Processing', in *Science and Technology in the Service of Conservation*, eds. N.S. Brommelle and G. Thomson, London 1982, pp. 159–61; D. Saunders, 'Colour Change Measurement by Digital Image Processing', *National Gallery Technical Bulletin*, 12, 1988, pp. 66–77, and D. Saunders and J. Cupitt, 'Image processing at the National Gallery: The VASARI project', *National Gallery Technical Bulletin*, 14 , 1993, pp. 72–85.
5. H. Chahine, J. Cupitt, D. Saunders and K. Martinez, 'Investigation and modelling of colour change in paintings during conservation treatment', in *Imaging the Past*, British Museum, Occasional Paper 114, eds. T Higgins, P.L. Main and J.L. Lang, London 1996.
6. A study of the changes in colour shown by a number of textiles during three months on display in a temporary exhibition is described in B.L. Ford, 'Monitoring Colour Change in Textiles on Display', *Studies in Conservation*, 37, 1992, pp. 1–11.
7. The Getty Conservation Institute have measured the colour of a number of areas at the surface of the wall paintings in the tomb of Nefertari before and after restoration. It is proposed that the same areas be monitored periodically in the future, see M. Schilling, 'The Color Measurement Program in the Tomb of Nefertari' in *Art and Eternity: The Nefertari Wall Paintings Conservation Project 1986–1992*, eds. M.A. Corzo and M. Afshar, Los Angeles 1993, pp. 83–93; and M.R. Schilling, 'Color Measurement

of the Wall Paintings in the Tomb of Nefertari', *Preprints of the International Council of Museums Committee for Conservation*, 10th triennial meeting, Washington DC 1993, pp. 42–9.

8. The CIE colour coordinates L^*, a^* and b^* correspond to three attributes of a colour. L^* represents the lightness of a colour on a scale from 0 (black) to 100 for a pure white. The a^* coordinate represents a red-green scale. A positive value for a^* indicates redness, while a negative value symbolises greenness. In the same way, b^* is a yellow-blue scale with positive values of b^* signifying yellowness. See Commission Internationale de l'Eclairage, 'Recommendations on uniform color spaces, color difference equations, psychometric color terms', Supplement No.2 to *CIE Publication No. 15 (E–2.3.1), 1971/(TC–1.3) (1978)*.

9. See notes 2 and 3.

10. See D. Saunders and J. Cupitt, 'Image processing at the National Gallery: The VASARI project', cited in note 4.

11. Since the electronic imaging system was first described in D. Saunders and J. Cupitt, 'Image processing at the National Gallery: The VASARI project', cited in note 4, a 12-bit camera has been installed which has improved the signal to noise ratio in the images. This, combined with a more efficient method for determining the white and black points for the image, has resulted in much greater colour accuracy in the final images. The average colour accuracy, calculated from the colour differences between measured and actual colours for the 24 colours in the Macbeth ColorChecker Chart, is now in the region of 1.5 – 2.0ΔE units.

12. The resampling is achieved by selecting matching points on the monochrome and colour images using a process analogous to that described in D. Saunders and J. Cupitt, 'Elucidating Reflectograms by superimposing Infra-red and Colour Images', *National Gallery Technical Bulletin*, 16, 1995, pp. 61–5. Although the correlation between the two images is often poor, making the selection of tie-points difficult, the accuracy required in this step is not great, since average colour values are to be calculated after resampling.

13. The circular mask generally contains around 1500 pixels. The L^*, a^* and b^* values of the corresponding pixels in the resampled colour image are summed and divided by the number of pixels in the mask to give average L^*, a^* and b^* values. When using a mask that simulates the shape and lightness of the spot, the L^*, a^* and b^* values in the colour image are weighted using the corresponding pixel in the mask. The weighting is taken into account when calculating the average colour coordinates.

14. Values of colour difference, ΔE, were calculated using the method described in British Standard 6923:1988, *British Standard method for calculation of small colour differences*, British Standards Institution, Milton Keynes 1988.

15. For example in *The Adoration of the Kings* by the Master of Liesborn the CIE data determined for point 1 on Plate 2 using a circular mask were: $L^* = 69.68$, $a^* = 0.39$, $b^* = 6.50$. The corresponding data for the mask which reflects the shape of the spot were: $L^* = 70.10$, $a^* = 0.44$, $b^* = 6.92$. The equivalent data for point 2, the point used as an example in Plate 1, were, circular mask: $L^* = 58.69$, $a^* = -9.90$, $b^* = 23.46$, spot mask: $L^* = 58.03$, $a^* = -10.07$, $b^* = 23.34$.

16. See note 11.

17. Examination of the robe to the left of *The Adoration of the Kings* by the Master of Liesborn under magnification suggested that the main pigment was vermilion. No sample was taken to confirm this identification. In the shadows a red lake glaze has been used, but measurement point 6 does not lie in an area to which such a glaze has been applied.

18. High-performance liquid chromatography was used to examine red lake samples from a number of the fragments from the dismembered altarpiece from the Benedictine Abbey at Liesborn (NG 256–261). Where dyestuff identification was possible, madder lake was found. See the article 'The Identification of Red Lake Pigment Dyestuffs and a Discussion of their Use' in this *Bulletin*.

19. D. Saunders and J. Kirby, 'Light-induced Colour Changes in Red and Yellow Lake Pigments', *National Gallery Technical Bulletin*, 15, 1994, pp. 79–97.

20. For the relatively homogeneous green area at point 6 on *The Roman Campagna, with the Claudian Aqueduct* by Corot the measured differences were: $\Delta L^* = 2.17$, $\Delta a^* = 0.00$, $\Delta b^* = -8.02$. Shifting the circular mask by up to 20% of its diameter gave minimum values of: $\Delta L^* = 2.17$, $\Delta a^* = -0.59$, $\Delta b^* = -8.00$.

21. For the inhomogeneous green bush at point 7 on *The Roman Campagna, with the Claudian Aqueduct* by Corot the measured differences were: $\Delta L^* = -5.82$, $\Delta a^* = 0.23$, $\Delta b^* = 11.34$. Shifting the circular mask by up to 20% of its diameter gave minimum values of: $\Delta L^* = -3.57$, $\Delta a^* = 0.06$, $\Delta b^* = 11.34$.

22. Examination of cross sections under the microscope by Ashok Roy confirmed the pigment identifications made when examining the painting under high magnification.

23. See note 19.

Analyses of Paint Media

RAYMOND WHITE AND JENNIFER PILC

A detailed Table of analytical results is presented here (pp. 96–99), with accompanying notes. In addition, the Table is prefaced with an introductory overview of the results and there is also included a brief note on experimental procedure.

Examination of the paint media used by painters of the Italian Schools has revealed that there was a gradual change from the use of egg tempera to the use of drying oils from the middle decades of the fifteenth century onwards. Painters naturally varied in their approach to the adoption of a paint medium with very different handling, drying and optical properties to those of egg. It is not unusual to find examples of both media used in the same painting and there are several different ways in which they could be employed. Several of the paintings examined, all but one produced in Florence during the years between the 1420s and the end of the century, contain both egg and drying oil and illustrate different approaches to the use of the two together.

The earliest example is particularly interesting from an art historical point of view. Two panels examined, *Saints Jerome and John the Baptist* (NG 5962) and *Saints Liberius(?) and Matthias* (NG 5963), are at present attributed jointly to Masaccio and his slightly older contemporary, Masolino. They were originally the front and back of a single panel, part of a double-sided triptych formerly in the Colonna Chapel in the church of Santa Maria Maggiore, Rome, but now dismembered; the central panels from the altarpiece are in the Museo di Capodimonte, Naples and those forming the other wing are in the Johnson Collection, Philadelphia Museum of Art. The altarpiece may date from between 1423 and 1428 (when Masaccio died), although the precise nature of

the presumed collaboration between the two artists is unclear.[1]

Stylistic differences between the two panels have led to the suggestion that Masaccio was largely responsible for *Saints Jerome and John the Baptist*, while *Saints Liberius(?) and Matthias* was mostly painted by Masolino. It was therefore particularly interesting that examination of the paint in several areas of the two panels revealed differences in the paint medium used. The handling of the flesh paint appeared markedly different and it was found that whereas egg tempera was used to paint Saint John's flesh, the paint of Saint Matthias's flesh contained egg enriched by the addition of a little drying oil. FTIR–microscopy indicated the presence of both protein and drying oil in discrete areas throughout the sample examined, suggesting that here an emulsion of drying oil in egg was used. Such a paint would have differed from ordinary egg tempera to the extent that it would be rather richer and could be manipulated more freely and with greater flexibility; it might allow a softer blending of individual brush strokes, if the artist so desired.

In the *Saints Jerome and John the Baptist* panel, Saint John's red cloak has been painted in egg tempera, possibly with a trace of drying oil added. In the companion panel, however, Saint Liberius's pinkish-cream cassock and Saint Matthias's olive-green robe have been painted in linseed oil. This is an extremely early instance of the use of linseed oil in a painting of any Italian School. The results as a whole may provide some corroborative evidence for the suggestion that the panels are by different hands, at least in part.[2] Masolino's presence in Florence is not recorded during the second decade of the fifteenth century and he is known to have been working in Hungary between 1425 and 1427.[3] If he had also had some contact with Northern European practice during his earlier period of absence, it is conceivable that he learned something of the use of drying oil at this time, if not later during his stay in Hungary.

The altarpiece of *The Trinity with Saints* (NG 727, 3162, 3230, 4428 and L15) was commissioned from Francesco Pesellino in 1455. On his death in 1457, Fra Filippo Lippi and his workshop in Prato completed the work by 1460. It is thought that Pesellino, who had probably trained in Lippi's workshop, was responsible for the overall design of the altarpiece and perhaps for the two figures on the left, while Lippi was responsible for the right-hand figures, the landscape and various other parts of the work, such as God's hands and the dove. The Lippi workshop is thought to have been responsible for the predella panels.[4] In the main panel, examination of paint from the left- and right-hand figures and parts of the sky and landscape showed that the medium used was egg containing an admixture of drying oil, similar to the paint used in the panel of *Saints Liberius(?) and Matthias* described above. The sky, however, was painted in egg tempera alone. In the paint used in the Trinity altarpiece for the robe of Saint Jerome (on the right), which was slightly richer in texture, the proportion of oil in the emulsion was correspondingly higher.[5] In this case, examination of the paint medium has thrown little light on the problems of attribution of the different parts of the picture: the same medium appears to have been used on the two sides of the painting, although not in the sky. The fact that the white paint of the rocks in the predella panel of Saint Jerome and the Lion (NG 4868.4) contains pure egg tempera may be significant, given that this part of the altarpiece is thought to have been produced by the Lippi workshop in Prato.

When egg tempera and drying oil are found in the same picture, it is perhaps most common to find egg tempera used for the underpaint with oil in the paint layers above, or egg used in certain areas of the painting – white, pale blue or flesh paint, for instance – and oil in others – reds and greens perhaps. The reason behind this may be purely visual: egg tempera gives a colder white, for example, and a paint surface with a slight sheen. The glazes of lake pigments and copper-containing green pigments used to model the shadows and folds of clothing are more effective in a medium of drying oil, however. A combination of the two methods of proceeding is found in *The Virgin and Child with Saint John* (NG 1412), painted by Filippino Lippi around 1475–80.[6] The pale blue sky was painted using egg tempera, while drying oils were used for the principal layers of the robes of Saint John and the Virgin. The Virgin's green sleeve lining, for which linseed oil was used, was underpainted in egg tempera, however. The red lake pigment (identified as lac lake)[7] used for Saint John's robe and the ultramarine used for the Virgin's robe are poor driers; accordingly the walnut oil used for the former and the linseed oil for the latter had both been heat pre-polymerised (partially, in the case of the walnut oil), presumably to assist drying.

Giovanni Antonio Boltraffio's *The Virgin and Child* (NG 728) presents a very much more complex case altogether, discussed at length elsewhere in this *Bulletin* (pp. 13–17).[8] A blackish underpaint, present in certain areas of the painting, such as the Virgin's robe, the green cloth of honour and the dark blue water in the background, contained egg tempera essentially, but with a trace of oil added; the paint above (where it was the original paint and not later restoration) contained oil, identified as walnut oil in the flesh of the Christ Child. However, a reddish isolating layer or *imprimitura* beneath the blackish underpaint, exposed in places where the dark-coloured paint has shrunk away, was also found to contain walnut oil. The use of a richer oil-containing *imprimitura* under the leaner egg tempera-containing underpaint is probably responsible for the shrinkage.

Of the sixteenth-century Italian paintings found to contain an oil medium, *The Adoration of the Kings* (NG 640) by the Ferrarese painter Girolamo da Carpi, and dating from about 1545–50, was interesting in that components of the medium appear to have been responsible for the severe wrinkling and reticulated appearance of the paint in certain areas of the picture. The paint of a tree trunk in the background, for example, has a markedly 'crocodiled' appearance, caused by the presence of a softwood pitch, identified by the presence of pyrolysis products derived from abietatriene acids, mixed with the walnut oil. This gives a brown colour, rather similar to that of asphaltum; like asphaltum, it tends to cause wrinkling and similar paint defects because it is liable to inhibit drying of the oil.[9] A softwood pitch was found in an orange-brown glaze, used to model the folds of an apostle's yellow robe in Cima da Conegliano's altarpiece, *The Incredulity of Saint Thomas* (NG 816), but in this case the paint is in very good condition, showing no drying faults.[10] It must be assumed that Girolamo da Carpi incorporated too much pitch in his mixture; even though the walnut oil used had been heat bodied to improve its drying properties, the paint dried poorly. It is worth noting that Cima used the more strongly drying linseed oil for his glaze. In his treatise on painting, published in 1587, Giovanni Battista Armenini suggests the use of 'the smoke of Greek pitch' as one of the pigments suitable for shadows on flesh (mummy and asphaltum being others), but with verdigris being added: this would aid drying.[11]

A rather similar, although less pronounced, defect is apparent in the right-hand kneeling figure's green cloak. The paint was found to contain walnut oil, with a small amount of pine resin. Examination of a fragment of the paint by FTIR–microscopy showed that the resin had only reacted with the copper-containing green pigment in one or two isolated areas: it was present essentially as a component of the paint medium rather than in the form of 'copper resinate'.[12] Further examination showed that less reticulated areas of the paint contained rather less pine resin. This suggests that the painter stirred a proportion of pine resin varnish, *vernice commune*, into the green paint, a little generously and carelessly perhaps, but rather as Armenini described for painting and glazing green draperies.[13]

The drying oils most frequently encountered in both sixteenth- and seventeenth-century paintings are linseed and walnut. Poppy oil, which, like walnut oil, is a semi-drying oil strictly speaking, is rather rarely encountered, although it has been identified in the painted wings of an altarpiece dating from 1525–30 in the church of Saint Lambert, Neerharen, Antwerp.[14] In the compilation of recipes made by the physician Theodore Turquet de Mayerne between 1620 and 1646, the properties of poppy oil are mentioned several times: it is said to be very pale, so particularly good for

white and blue, and it does not spoil the colours.[15] Philippe de La Hyre (writing at the beginning of the eighteenth century, but perhaps referring back to the procedures in use during the years around 1660, when he was training) describes poppy oil as being paler than walnut oil, but says it was used only for small works, where it could 'contribute to the beauty and vivacity of the colours'.[16] In the two seventeenth-century French paintings in the National Gallery collection in which it has been identified, it occurs in white or light coloured paint. In an earlier study, poppy oil was identified in the white ermine on the Cardinal's red robe in Philippe de Champaigne's *Cardinal Richelieu* (NG 1449), of about 1637.[17] The present examination revealed the presence of linseed oil in the paint of a shadow in the fold of the same red robe, but what could be either walnut oil or a mixture of linseed and poppy oils in the grey paint of the architecture. In the circumstances, the latter possibility is far more likely; probably the artist ground his lead white in poppy oil, but used linseed oil for other pigments, resulting in a mixture of oils in the grey paint. Poppy oil was also found used for the sitter's white cuff in the *Portrait of a Man* (NG 2929), attributed to Gabriel Revel, whereas linseed oil was found in the red glaze on the sleeve.

The National Gallery collection includes several paintings by Nicolas Poussin and by artists in his circle, those by Poussin himself dating largely from his two periods of activity in Rome, from 1624 to 1640 and again from 1642 until his death in 1665. He returned briefly to Paris in 1640–2. A notable characteristic of his studio practice is the care he appears to have taken over most aspects of his work; little appears to have been left to chance. This careful approach seems to have extended to his painting technique, which, as far as the paint medium used is concerned, appears very sound. The painter used linseed or walnut oil, often heat pre-polymerised (which gives the paint extra body as well as improving drying); heat-bodied linseed oil was used in the lime green paint of foliage on the right of *A Bacchanalian Revel before a Term of Pan* (NG 62), dating from about 1630–4, for example, while heat-bodied walnut oil was used for green foliage paint in *Landscape with a Man washing his Feet at a Fountain* (NG 40), of about 1648. There appears to be no particular preference for employing walnut oil with white or blue pigments, for which it was traditionally used.

A few seventeenth-century artists were in the habit of adding a small amount of pine resin to their paint, either for particular colours or in general, to add increased gloss and transparency to the paint.[18] This would be particularly effective in giving increased depth to areas of shadow or in glazing draperies and it is not uncommon to find an addition of resin to the paint for this purpose. Philippe de Champaigne added a little pine resin to the linseed oil used for the glaze of Cardinal Richelieu's red robe, while pine resin and mastic were present in the medium used in the glaze on the sitter's coat in the portrait attributed to Gabriel Revel. Poussin seems not to have followed this practice. The only exception is the early, and unfinished, *Nurture of Bacchus* (NG 39), dated about 1627, where a trace of pine resin was present in the cream-coloured sky above the horizon. Of the painters in Poussin's immediate circle, his brother-in-law, Gaspard Dughet, seems also to have used conventional linseed oil on the whole; only in the *Landscape in the Roman Campagna (Tivoli?)* (NG 161) were traces of pine resin also found. (Examination of the paint samples by FTIR–microscopy ruled out the possibility of contamination from an old varnish layer.) In view of Poussin's apparent preference for a simple drying oil medium, the results obtained from *Bacchanalian Festival with Silenus* (NG 42), dating from about 1635–6 and only attributed to the artist, were particularly interesting. Both the sky and foliage were found to have been painted in linseed oil, but in both cases a little resin had been added to the oil, pine resin alone in the case of the sky, mastic and pine resin in the foliage.

By the late eighteenth and nineteenth centuries, literary sources suggest that the incorporation of various types of varnish into drying oils was not uncommon.[19] The disastrous effects of the inappropriate or ill-considered use of some of these – the notorious megilp (essentially equal parts of linseed oil, prepared with lead driers, and mastic varnish shaken together) condemned by many writers – have been much discussed, ever since the contemporaries of Sir Joshua Reynolds lamented the results of his

experimenting with his materials.[20] However, in more cautious hands, varnish-containing media gave perfectly stable and lasting paint films. Paul Delaroche used a medium consisting of heat pre-polymerised linseed oil mixed with mastic varnish for several areas of his painting *The Execution of Lady Jane Grey* (NG 1909), dated 1833, including the red glaze pattern of the brown brocade dress on the seated attendant's lap and the executioner's black coat. The paint of this coat has retained the brushwork to an extent that is not usually seen in black paint, the extra body being provided by the mastic-containing medium used. Other areas of the painting – the brown paint of the brocade dress, Lady Jane's white dress – were painted in ordinary drying oils, linseed oil for the former, walnut for the latter. One of the painting varnishes described by Mérimée in his book of 1830 is the so-called *vernis des Anglais*, which had a jelly-like consistency and consisted of mastic and linseed oil alone (without beeswax or any other additional components); possibly Delaroche used something of this type.[21] The picture is very thinly and carefully painted; despite the fact that, at one stage in its history, it suffered flood damage, the paint is sound and in remarkably good condition.[22]

J.M.W. Turner, Delaroche's contemporary, was a painter who could be described as throwing caution to the winds as far as his use of materials was concerned. He is reported as having used varnish mixtures, beeswax and spermaceti wax in his media as well as conventional drying oils;[23] he is also recorded as having worked extensively on his paintings on the so-called 'varnishing days' at the Royal Academy or British Institution, when artists were permitted to retouch or varnish their works immediately before the opening of the exhibition.[24] For this he is said to have used watercolours, or, according to John Ruskin, dry pigments applied in water, glue or whatever came to hand, then varnished.[25]

Turner's *The Fighting 'Temeraire' tugged to her last Berth to be broken up, 1838* (NG 524), the subject of a National Gallery *Making and Meaning* exhibition in 1995, has never been cleaned; the results of examination of the surface layers in some areas of the painting were therefore particularly interesting.[26] The salmon-pink paint of the sunset contained heat pre-polymerised walnut oil (needless to say, Turner did not restrict his use of walnut oil to white or pale colours); the paint also contained Sumatra benzoin. From the sixteenth century onwards, recipes can be found for varnishes for delicate, decorative objects that will not be subjected to handling, using the alcohol-soluble benzoins.[27] The varnish dries almost immediately after painting and would thus permit the rapid application of layer upon layer of paint, applied very thinly, without picking up pigment from the layer below, as the artist sought to emphasise or to modify some aspect of the painted surface, perhaps so that it would not lose by the sudden comparison with the works of other artists that had come to hang nearby for the duration of the exhibition. During sampling it was suspected that more than one layer of paint was present; as it is unlikely that a benzoin-containing spirit varnish could be mixed satisfactorily with walnut oil, it seems that the varnish was used for the final touches of salmon pink, over the oil paint. It is less likely, although not impossible, that the artist worked without a conventional medium for these last touches, then applied the spirit varnish over the top.

Turner used walnut oil, sometimes heat-bodied, sometimes not, as his principal medium, but the results of analysis show a range of resins also present, with the oil, in different areas of the painting: pine resin and mastic in the brownish-black shadow of the buoy; pine resin and a dammar in the mustard-coloured reflection of the sun in the sea; a still unidentified triterpenoid resin in the white impasto of a cloud. These probably indicate the use of the various varnishes, megilp and other proprietary products, in which Turner showed a great interest and is also known to have purchased, mixed into the paint on the palette.[28] The presence of a non-drying fat in the white paint of the clouds suggests something (possibly tallow – the material could not be precisely characterised) added as a plasticiser to give some softness to their surface texture. Although there are occasional references to the addition of soap to oil paint, this could equally well be some other household material (like salad oil or dripping) Turner happened to have to hand.[29]

More technical and detailed information concerning the samples and their analyses can be found in the notes to the Table, below.

Note on an Improved Analytical Procedure

Most of the analytical results presented here have been obtained using a new, single-stage and improved derivatisation procedure. Reference was made to this in last year's *Bulletin*.

Thermal degradation of quaternary ammonium salts of carboxylic acids in the heated injection port of a gas-chromatograph has been known to produce *in situ* methylation of such acids and has been utilised for three decades. However, the method has a serious drawback in that with the usual reagents, tetramethyl- and trimethylphenylammonium hydroxides, thermolysis temperatures are high and the alkalinity of the reagents lead to base-induced isomerisations of the more labile functional features of a molecule (for example double bonds, hydroxyl groups and others).[30] The trifluoromethyl homologue of the latter reagent, that is, *m*-(trifluoromethyl)phenyl-trimethyl-ammonium hydroxide, or trimethyl(α,α,α-trifluoro-*m*-tolyl)ammonium hydroxide – abbreviated to TMTFTH – has been tested in this laboratory and has been found to perform very well in the conversion of labile fatty and terpenoid acids to their methyl esters. In addition, this reagent is able to effect a conversion of glycerides to methyl esters of their component acids. This appears to be the result of the reduced alkalinity of this reagent, in comparison to those mentioned above, and the superior properties of dimethyl(trifluoro)toluidine as a leaving group, resulting in a lower thermolysis temperature.

TMTFTH is commercially available and is readily made in the laboratory in methanolic solution by a slight modification of the method reported by MacGee and Allen.[31] Experimental details appear below.[32]

Analyses of Paint Media

Artist	Picture	Date
EARLIER ITALIAN SCHOOLS		
Lorenzo Monaco	*Adoring Saints* NG 216	probably 1407–9
	The Coronation of the Virgin NG 1897	probably 1407–9
Attributed to **Masaccio** and **Masolino**	*Saints Jerome and John the Baptist* NG 5962	probably between 1423 and 1428
	Saints Liberius(?) and Matthias NG 5963	probably between 1423 and 1428
Follower of **Fra Angelico**	*The Annunciation* NG 1406	probably about 1450
Francesco Pesellino	*The Trinity with Saints* NG 727	1455–60
	Predella of the Trinity with Saints Altarpiece NG 4868.4	1455–60
Filippino Lippi	*The Virgin and Child with Saint John* NG 1412	1480
Giovanni Antonio Boltraffio	*The Virgin and Child* NG 728	probably about 1493–9
Leonardo da Vinci	*The Virgin of the Rocks (The Virgin with the Infant Saint John adoring the Infant Christ accompanied by an Angel)* NG 1093	about 1508
After **Luini**	*Saint Catherine* NG 3936	early 16th century
Vincenzo Catena	*Portrait of the Doge, Andrea Gritti* NG 5751	probably 1523 to 1531
Girolamo da Carpi	*The Adoration of the Kings* NG 640	probably about 1545–50

Sample	Medium	P/S	Oil type	Note
1. Red lake paint of left-hand saint's robe	Egg			33
2. Mordant of lost gilding of pattern of Saint Peter's robe	Egg, possibly glue			
1. Blue of Christ's robe	Egg			34
2. Faded paint of Mary's robe	Egg			
1. Red shadow of fold of Saint John's cloak	Egg (+ trace of oil?)			35
2. Flesh paint of Saint John's right shoulder	Egg			
1. Pinkish-cream paint of Pope's cassock	Oil	1.7	Linseed	36
2. Olive-green paint of the cloak of Saint Mathias	Oil	1.2	Linseed	
3. Pale flesh paint from the back of Saint Mathias's neck	Egg + some oil			
1. Adhesive or mordant of gilding, trimmings of Virgin's right sleeve	Glue			37
2. Flesh paint of angel's neck	Egg			
3. Pale pink of angel's dress	Egg			
1. Green of trees on horizon	Egg + some oil			38
2. Yellow of inside of cloak of left-hand saint	Egg + some oil			
1. White rocks , upper right-hand corner	Egg			
1. Pale blue sky	Egg			39
2a. Green lining of Virgin's sleeve, principal layer	Oil	1.5	Linseed	
2b. Underpaint to above	Egg			
3. Red lake glaze of Saint John's cloak	Oil	2.5	Walnut	
4. Blue of the sleeve of the Virgin's robe	Oil	1.2	Linseed	
1. Red paint of Virgin's right sleeve	Oil + egg			40
2. Blue-black water in background, rocky scene, left side.	Oil			
3. Flesh paint, Christ Child's left leg	Oil	3.1	Walnut	
4. Black contracted underpaint, exposed at left-hand edge of green backcloth	Egg + oil			
5. Red-brown underpaint, exposed on Virgin's finger	Oil	2.1	Walnut	
6. Exposed black underpaint from edge of cuff of Virgin's right arm	Egg + oil			
1. Brownish-black paint of rocks, right-hand side	Oil	2.2	Walnut	41
2. Red-brown *imprimitura* layer (beneath sample 1)	Oil	2.1	Walnut	
3. Blue-black of angel's robe	Oil	2.5	Walnut	
4. Green leaf, lower edge	Oil	2.5	Walnut	
5. Pale bluish-green sky, between rocks at top	Oil	2.5	Walnut	
1. Brown paint of shadow of wheel	Oil	1.9	Linseed	
2. Dark green background	Oil	2.0	Linseed	
3. Red paint of Saint Catherine's right, upper sleeve	Oil	1.9	Linseed	
1. Dark red glaze of cap	Oil	1.6	Linseed	42
2. Flesh paint of neck	Oil	1.8	Linseed	
3. Yellow brocade, highlight of fold	Oil	1.6	Linseed	
4. Flesh paint of left forefinger	Oil	1.8	Linseed	
1. Brownish-black, heavily 'crocodiled' paint of tree trunk, mid-background scene	Oil + softwood pitch	2.7	Walnut	43
2. Green glaze-like paint of cloak of right-hand kneeling figure	Oil + pine resin	2.1	Walnut	

Artist	Picture	Date
FRENCH SCHOOLS		
Nicolas Poussin	*The Nurture of Bacchus* NG 39	about 1627
	A Bacchanalian Revel before a Term of Pan NG 62	1630–4
	The Adoration of the Golden Calf NG 5597	by 1634
	Landscape in the Roman Campagna with a Man scooping Water NG 6390	about 1637–8
	Landscape in the Roman Campagna NG 6391	about 1639–40
	Landscape with a Man killed by a Snake NG 5763	1648
	Landscape with a Man washing his Feet at a Fountain NG 40	about 1648
	The Annunciation NG 5472	1657
Attributed to **Nicolas Poussin**	*Bacchanalian Festival with Silenus* NG 42	1635–6
After **Nicolas Poussin**	*The Holy Family with Saints Elizabeth and John* NG 1422	after 1710
Philippe de Champaigne	*Cardinal Richelieu* NG 1449	about 1637
Gaspard Dughet	*Landscape in the Roman Campagna (near Albano?)* NG 68	about 1670
	Landscape in the Roman Campagna NG 98	about 1670
	Landscape in the Roman Campagna (Tivoli?) NG 161	about 1670
Attributed to **Crescenzio Onofri**	*Landscape with Figures* NG 2723	probably 1670–1712
Attributed to **Gabriel Revel**	*Portrait of a Man* NG 2929	about 1675
Pierre Mignard	*The Marquise de Seignelay and Two of her Children* NG 2967	1691
Paul Delaroche	*The Execution of Lady Jane Grey* NG 1909	1833
BRITISH SCHOOLS		
Joseph Mallord William Turner	*The Fighting 'Temeraire' tugged to her last Berth to be broken up, 1838* NG 524	before 1839

Sample	Medium	P/S	Oil type	Note
1. Dark grey of added(?) strip	Oil	2.2	Walnut	44
2. Cream paint of distant sky	Oil + resin	1.6	Linseed	
1. Lime-green impasto paint of leaf, right-hand corner	Oil	1.6	Linseed	45
2. Blue sky, same area	Oil			
1. Blue robe of left-hand female figure	Oil			46
2. Yellow highlight of sleeve, woman seated with child	Oil			
1. Pinkish-white sky	Oil	2.2	Walnut	
2. Brownish-green leaves	Oil	1.7	Linseed	
1. Peach-coloured rock	Oil	1.7	Linseed	
2. Brownish-green leaf	Oil	1.7	Linseed	
1. Blue sky	Oil	1.4	Linseed	
2. Green foliage	Oil	1.8	Linseed	
1. Blue sky	Oil	1.5	Linseed	47
2. Green foliage, right-hand edge	Oil	2.3	Walnut	
1. White of angel's hem	Oil	2.4	Walnut	48
2. Yellow of Mary's shawl	Oil	2.2	Walnut	
1. Pale blue sky	Oil + some resin	1.6	Linseed	49
2. Green foliage	Oil + some resin	1.2	Linseed	
1. Light brown floor in background	Oil			50
1. Grey paint of moulding of plinth of enjoined pilaster	Oil	2.7	Poppy + Linseed?	51
2. Wine-red shadow of fold of robe	Oil + resin	1.5	Linseed	
1. Brown-green foliage	Oil	1.5	Linseed	52
2. Blue sky	Oil	1.5	Linseed	
1. Blue sky	Oil	1.8	Linseed	
2. Mustard highlight in path	Oil	1.5	Linseed	
1. Blue sky	Oil + some resin	1.8	Linseed	
2. Lime-green foliage	Oil + some resin	1.7	Linseed	
1. Pale blue sky	Oil	2.4	Walnut	
2. Cream-coloured paint of cloud	Oil	1.2	Linseed	
1. Red glaze paint of sitter's right sleeve	Oil + resin	1.2	Linseed	53
2. White of sitter's right cuff	Oil + resin	3.8	Poppy	
1. Pale cream paint of distant sky	Oil	3.0	Walnut	54
2. Red glaze paint of fold of drape, right-hand side	Oil	3.1	Walnut	
3. Blue sky	Oil	2.4	Walnut	
1. Upper, pale ground	Oil	2.4	Walnut	55
2. Lower, darker ground	Oil	1.8	Linseed	
3. White paint of Lady Jane's left sleeve	Oil	2.5	Walnut	
4. Black paint of executioner's right sleeve	Oil + resin	1.4	Linseed	
5. Brownish background colour of patterned dress over lap of fainting attendant	Oil	1.8	Linseed	
6. Red lake paint of pattern of dress on left-hand female attendant's lap	Oil + resin	1.7	Linseed	
1. Impasto paint of white cloud	Oil + resin	3.0	Walnut	56
2. Salmon-pink sunset	Oil + benzoin	3.0	Walnut	
3. Brownish-black buoy	Oil + resin	3.2	Walnut	
4. Mustard reflection of sun on sea	Oil + resin	2.6	Walnut	

Notes and References

1. J. Dunkerton, S. Foister, D. Gordon and N. Penny, *Giotto to Dürer: Early Renaissance Painting in the National Gallery*, New Haven and London 1991, pp. 252–4; P. Joannides, *Masaccio and Masolino: A Complete Catalogue*, London 1993, pp. 72–9, 414–22.

2. In one of the two panels in the Johnson Collection, Philadelphia, *Saints Peter and Paul* (cat. 23), egg tempera appears to have been used for the hands and feet while an egg-oil mixture was used elsewhere: see C. Strehlke and M. Tucker, 'The Santa Maria Maggiore Altarpiece, new observations', *Arte Cristiana*, LXXV, 719, March/April 1987, pp. 105–24; Joannides, ibid., p. 420.

3. For Masolino's early training and period in Hungary, 1425–7 (of which little is known), see Joannides, ibid., pp. 25–6, 31–2, 37–45, 153.

4. M. Davies, *National Gallery Catalogues: The Earlier Italian Schools*, London 1961 (1986 reprint), pp. 414–9; J. Ruda, *Fra Filippo Lippi: Life and Work, with a Complete Catalogue*, London 1993, pp. 449–52.

5. The analysis of this paint, and that from several other areas of the painting, was reported in an earlier issue of this *Bulletin*: see J. Mills and R. White, 'Paint Media Analyses', *National Gallery Technical Bulletin*, 13, 1989, pp. 69–71.

6. J. Dunkerton and A. Roy, 'The Materials of a Group of late Fifteenth-century Florentine Panel Paintings', in this *Bulletin*, pp. 21–31.

7. J. Kirby and R. White, 'The Identification of Red Lake Pigment Dyestuffs', in this *Bulletin*, pp. 56–80, especially p. 80.

8. L. Keith and A. Roy, 'Giampietrino, Boltraffio and the Influence of Leonardo', in this *Bulletin*, pp. 5–19, especially pp. 14–15.

9. R. White, 'Brown and Black Organic Glazes, Pigments and Paints', *National Gallery Technical Bulletin*, 10, 1986, pp. 58–71, especially pp. 65–7.

10. J. Dunkerton and A. Roy, 'The Technique and Restoration of Cima's "The Incredulity of S. Thomas"', *National Gallery Technical Bulletin*, 10, 1986, pp. 4–27, especially p. 17.

11. G.B. Armenini, *De' veri precetti della pittura*, Ravenna 1587, p. 124: '... il fumo di pece greca, il quale perche egli non hà corpo, s'incorpora benissimo col verderame ben macinato con oglio prima, del quale vi se ne mette un terzo & due di fumo ...' Armenini also recommends the addition of a little varnish, probably the *vernice commune* (essentially a varnish made with pine resin and oil) to which he refers elsewhere (p. 126). Some recipes for *vernice commune* include Greek pitch as an ingredient: see, for example, L. Fioravanti, *Del compendio dei secreti rationali...*, Venice 1564, p. 172. The resulting varnish would undoubtedly be very dark in colour.

12. J. Pilc and R. White, 'The Application of FTIR–microscopy to the Analysis of Paint Binders in Easel Paintings', *National Gallery Technical Bulletin*, 16, 1995, pp. 73–84, especially p. 82.

13. Armenini, 1587, cited in note 11, p. 126.

14. J. Sanyova, 'Etude scientifique des techniques picturales des retables anversois', *Antwerpse retabels, 15de–16de eeuw*, exhibition catalogue, edited by H. Nieuwdorp; 2 vols. (Vol. I. Catalogue; Vol. II. Essays), Antwerp 1993, Vol. II, pp. 151–64, especially p. 155.

15. T. T. de Mayerne, *Pictoria, sculptoria, tinctoria et quae subalternarum artium spectantia*, 1620–46 (British Library (British Museum) MS. Sloane 2052): edition annotated by J.A. van de Graaf, *Het de Mayerne Manuscript als Bron voor de Schildertechniek van de Barock*, diss., Utrecht 1958, no. 86a p. 178; no. 90, p. 180.

16. P. de La Hyre, 'Traité de la pratique de peinture', *Mémoires de l'Académie Royale des Sciences depuis 1666 jusqu'à 1699*, IX, Paris 1730, pp. 637–730, especially p. 707: 'mais ce n'a été que pour de petits ouvrages, où ils ont recherché tout ce qui pouvoit contribuer à la beauté et à la vivacité des couleurs'.

17. J.S. Mills and R. White, 'The Gas Chromatographic Examination of Paint Media. Some Examples of Medium Identification in Paintings by Fatty Acid Analysis', *Conservation and Restoration of Pictorial Art*, edited by N. Brommelle and P. Smith, London 1976, pp. 72–7.

18. R. White and J. Kirby, 'Rembrandt and his Circle: Seventeenth-Century Dutch Paint Media Re-examined', *National Gallery Technical Bulletin*, 15, 1994, pp. 64–77, especially pp. 71–3.

19. See, for example, J.F. Watin, *L'Art du peintre, doreur, vernisseur*, 3rd edn., Paris 1776 (1st edn. 1772), pp. 187–314; J.-F.-L. Mérimée, *De la peinture à l'huile*, Paris 1830 (facsimile reprint, Puteaux 1981), pp. 65–91 (the English edition of this book was published in 1839); L. Carlyle, *A Critical Analysis of Artists' Handbooks, Manuals and Treatises on Oil Painting Published in Britain between 1800–1900: With Reference to Selected Eighteenth Century Sources*, Ph.D. dissertation, Courtauld Institute of Art, University of London, 1991, pp. 42–189; L. Carlyle, 'Varnish Preparation and Practice 1750–1850', *Turner's Painting Techniques in Context*, 1995, edited by J.H. Townsend, London 1995, pp. 21–8.

20. L. Carlyle and A. Southall, 'No Short Mechanic Road to Fame: The Implications of Certain Artists' Materials for the Durability of British Painting: 1770–1840', in R. Hamlyn, *Robert*

Vernon's Gift: British Art for the Nation 1847, exhibition catalogue, London 1993, pp. 21–6; A. Southall, 'Turner's Contemporaries: Their Materials, Practices and Opinions', *Turner's Painting Techniques in Context, 1995*, ibid., pp. 12–20; M.K. Talley, '"All good pictures crack"; Sir Joshua Reynolds's practice and studio', in *Reynolds*, edited by N. Penny, exhibition catalogue, Paris/London 1985–6, pp. 55–70, especially pp. 55–6, 62–4, 67–8.

21. Mérimée, 1830, cited in note 19, pp. 70–1.

22. J. Kirby and A. Roy, 'Paul Delaroche: A Case Study of Academic Painting', *Historical Painting Techniques, Materials and Studio Practice*: Preprints of a Symposium, University of Leiden, the Netherlands, 26-29 June 1995, edited by A. Wallert, E. Hermens and M. Peek, Malibu 1995, pp. 166–75, especially p. 172.

23. See, for example, J.H. Townsend, 'Painting Techniques and Materials of Turner and Other British Artists 1775–1875', *Historical Painting Techniques*, ibid., pp. 176–85; J.H. Townsend, 'Turner's Use of Materials, and Implications for Conservation', *Turner's Painting Techniques in Context, 1995*, cited in note 19, pp. 5–11; M. Odlyha, 'The Role of Thermoanalytical Techniques in the Characterisation of Samples from Turner's "The Opening of the Wallhalla"', ibid., pp. 29–34; J.J. Boon, J. Pureveen, D. Rainford and J.H. Townsend, '"The Opening of the Wallhalla, 1842": Studies on the Molecular Signature of Turner's Paint by Direct Temperature–resolved Mass Spectrometry (DTMS)', ibid., pp. 35–45.

24. There are several references to Turner's activities on varnishing days in M. Butlin and E. Joll, *The Paintings of J.M.W. Turner*, 2nd edn., London and New Haven 1985.

25. Ibid.; see also Townsend, 'Turner's Use of Materials, and Implications for Conservation', cited in note 23, p. 10.

26. J. Egerton, *Making and Meaning: Turner,'The Fighting Temeraire'*, with a technical examination of the painting by M. Wyld and A. Roy, exhibition catalogue, London 1995, pp. 121–3, 132.

27. *Segreti diversi*; the Marciana manuscript (Venice, Biblioteca Marciana, MS Ital. IV 48, sixteenth century) in M.P. Merrifield, *Original Treatises dating from the XIIth to the XVIIIth centuries on the Arts of Painting*, London 1849 (Dover reprint, New York and London 1967), Vol. II, nos. 394, 396–7, pp. 628–31; P.F. Tingry, *The Painter and Varnisher's Guide ...*, 2nd edn., London 1816, pp. 2, 59 (the material is mixed with other resins in this recipe); A.-M. Tripier-Deveaux, *Traité théorique et pratique sur l'art de faire les vernis*, Paris 1845, pp. 27–9. It should be said that benzoin is barely mentioned in sources at this time; it may have featured anonymously in one of the proprietary products available (see Carlyle, 1991, cited in note 19, p. 116) or the artist may have prepared it himself.

28. Townsend, 'Turner's Use of Materials, and Implications for Conservation', cited in note 23, pp. 7–10. For the use of Canada balsam see Carlyle, 1991, cited in note 19, pp. 114–15.

29. For the use of soap see Carlyle, ibid., pp. 157–8.

30. K. B. Anderson and R. E. Winans, 'Nature and Fate of Natural Resins in the Geosphere. 1. Evaluation of Pyrolysis-Gas Chromatography/Mass Spectrometry for the Analysis of Natural Resins and Resinites', *Analytical Chemistry*, 63, 1991, pp. 2901-8.

31. J. MacGee and K. G. Allen, 'Preparation of Methyl Esters from the Saponifiable Fatty Acids in Small Biological Specimens for Gas-Liquid Chromatographic Analysis', *Journal of Chromatography*, 100, 1974, pp. 35-42.

32. A 10 or 20 microlitre aliquot of a 5% methanolic solution of TMTFTH is added to the paint fragment in a 100 microlitre tapered reaction vial. The vial is sealed and heated to 60° Celsius for 5 hours; it is then allowed to stand for 2 hours after centrifugation. A 1 microlitre aliquot is injected onto a quartz HT5 (mixed carborane-siloxane stationary phase) capillary column, with an injection port temperature of 200° Celsius. Slow injection is not required and the chromatogram yields information on both combined and free acids in the form of their methyl esters. The first run of the day should be an aliquot of the methanolic reagent alone to condition both injector and column.

33. The mordant appeared to be proteinaceous and was contaminated by some paint beneath. The result of analysis by GC–MS indicated the presence of egg tempera lipids, mainly from the orange-yellow paint itself. A fragment of reasonably pure mordant showed little more than background lipids by GC–MS and indicates the use of glue. For materials and techniques of early Italian gilding, see D. Bomford, J. Dunkerton, D. Gordon and A. Roy, with contributions from J. Kirby in *Art in the Making: Italian Painting Before 1400*, exhibition catalogue, London 1989/90, pp. 21–4, 43–8.

34. The sample was taken from a relatively thick spot of paint; a cholestadien-7-one component ($m/z = 382$ (M$^+$), $m/z = 174$ (B$^+$)) derived from cholesterol originally present, which usually disappears with the passage of time, was still just detectable.

35. Both paints from this work were bound with egg tempera; there was some indication that sample 1 might also contain a minor addition of drying oil.

36. Pinkish-cream and olive-green paints were found to contain oil, with no evidence for the presence of egg tempera medium. Sample 3, flesh paint,

contained essentially egg tempera medium, but also some drying oil. These results point to an unusually early use of oil medium for Italy.

37. These results represent further sampling during the course of conservation treatment on this work. Previous media results were reported in R. White and J. Pilc, 'Analyses of Paint Media', *National Gallery Technical Bulletin*, 16, 1995, pp. 86–7.

38. Both green and yellow paints gave indications of egg tempera medium, but with a little drying oil. There was no suggestion that the oil and tempera were other than in the same paint layer. These results confirm the general conclusions reached in an earlier study reported in J. Mills and R. White, 'Paint Media Analyses', *National Gallery Technical Bulletin*, 13, 1989, pp. 69–71.

39. The red glaze paint of Saint John's cloak (sample 3) was identified as containing partially heat-bodied walnut oil, by GC–MS. Similarly, sample 4 (blue robe) was found to contain heat-bodied linseed oil.

40. In general, the layer structures of the paints sampled from this work were rather complex. FTIR–microscopy and GC–MS of partially separated layers of sample 1, red paint from the Virgin's right sleeve, indicated the presence of a dark underpaint in egg with, possibly, some drying oil too. Above this there appeared to be a red lake paint in drying oil (walnut oil, not heat-bodied). Above this was a resinous layer (mastic resin) and finally a red lake overpaint bound, essentially, by mastic resin. Sample 2 of blue/black water was similarly complex. It was not possible to separate the layers for GC–MS. The result obtained represents an average for both the dark underpaint and blue/black paint layers. FTIR would suggest that there is egg tempera in the dark, blackish underpaint (possibly with a little oil), while a thin reddish-brown isolating layer and a blue paint are in oil medium. A sample of flesh paint from Christ's leg did not appear to have any black underpaint and was found to contain walnut oil, there being no evidence for egg tempera. A sample of the black underpaint itself, from an area of the backcloth where the principal paint layer had flaked away, appeared to contain a mixture of egg tempera and some drying oil. This layer seemed to have undergone shrinkage and exhibited a very coarse craquelure. A reddish-brown *imprimitura* beneath the black underpaint, sampled from an area where it had been exposed as a result of shrinkage of the black paint above, contained walnut oil alone. For a fuller account see Keith and Roy, cited in note 8, pp. 14–15.

41. GC–MS indicated the use of heat-bodied walnut oil in each sample from this work.

42. GC–MS indicated the use of heat-bodied linseed oil in each sample from this work.

43. Brownish-black paint was identified as containing heat-bodied walnut oil, together with abietatriene acids and their pyrolysis products, such as retene and nor-abietatrienes. The latter components point to the inclusion of a softwood pitch or resin tar within the drying oil medium; much as in the case of asphaltum or bitumen, these have contributed to the paint film defects observed. Sample 2, green glaze-like paint, which exhibited some measure of 'reticulation', was found to contain heat-bodied walnut oil with some pine resin. FTIR–microscopy gave no indication that the pigment was 'copper resinate', although in some isolated areas there had been some interaction between the copper pigment and the resinous addition to the drying oil medium. Interestingly, a sample taken from a less reticulated area of the green paint, though based on the same components, appeared to have a somewhat lower proportion of resin present

44. GC–MS gave indications of heat pre-polymerisation in the case of grey paint from the added strip. The cream sky paint contained a little pine resin in addition to the linseed oil.

45. The linseed oil employed as binder for the lime-green paint had been heat-bodied. FTIR–microscopy indicated that a fragment of blue sky paint, inadvertently sampled with the green leaf paint, was bound with drying oil.

46. Gas-chromatographic results for the medium of samples examined earlier were reported in J. Mills and R. White, 'Analyses of Paint Media', *National Gallery Technical Bulletin*, 3, 1979, pp. 66–7. Two further fragments were sampled in the current study for examination by FTIR–microscopy. Both contained drying oil as paint binding medium.

47. GC–MS showed that the green paint of the foliage contained heat-bodied walnut oil as binder.

48. Both samples appeared to contain heat pre-polymerised oil; the yellow paint's binding medium appeared to have undergone partial heat-bodying, or was a mixture of bodied and non-bodied oils.

49. The green foliage paint, though based on linseed oil, also contained a little pine and mastic resins, but there was no indication of the use of 'copper resinate' here. The blue sky contained a minor addition of pine resin alone.

50. FTIR–microscopy was used for this examination only.

51. An earlier study, using GC, was reported in Mills and White, 1976, cited in note 17. In view of the use of poppy oil and the presence of linseed oil in the red fold of the robe, it seems likely that the palmitic/stearic ester ratio for the grey paint results from the admixture of poppy-seed and linseed oils, rather than from the use of

walnut oil. The red lake paint also contained a little pine resin.

52. In the case of NG 161, a minor addition of pine resin to the linseed oil binder was detected; FTIR–microscopy established that this was not due to contaminating fragments of varnish. This may account for the slightly more transparent quality of the paint in areas of this work.

53. The red paint, bound in pre-polymerised linseed oil essentially, was found to contain both pine and mastic resins in addition. These resins were also present in the medium of the white cuff paint, which consisted principally of heat-bodied poppy oil.

54. In the case of the cream and red paints the walnut oil had been heat-bodied.

55. See Kirby and Roy, 1995, cited in note 22. Of the two ground layers, the lower, darker one is probably a commercial ground prepared with linseed oil; its darker colour is solely due to wax/resin lining of the canvas. The upper, lighter ground was prepared using walnut oil and is likely to be a studio-prepared ground. The white paint of Lady Jane's left sleeve contained walnut oil; there was no evidence for resin within the body of the medium, unlike the rich, 'bodied' black paint of the executioner's coat, bound with heat-bodied linseed oil into which a little mastic resin had been mixed. The paint showed no signs of the usual drying problems that frequently accrue with black paint and GC–MS indicated the absence of bitumen, asphaltum and heavily 'pitched' softwood. The cochineal lake glaze of the brocade dress on the attendant's lap also contained a mixture of heat-bodied linseed oil with the addition of some mastic resin.

56. See Egerton, 1995, cited in note 26. Sample 1 (white impasto) contained a trace of a triterpenoid resin in addition to walnut oil; the source is uncertain, but it is probably a Dipterocarpaceous resin and certainly not from the genus *Pistacia*. Some non-drying fats – probably tallow – were also present. Sample 2 (salmon-pink sunset) proved quite unusual. FTIR–microscopy indicated the presence of some drying oil, but other bands suggested that some form of resin might be present. GC–MS revealed the presence of walnut oil. The drying components did not appear to have suffered any dilution by non-drying oils or fats in this case and the oil had been heat pre-polymerised. Other minor components were also present. Some of these were identified as derived from benzoic acid, methoxy analogues and cinnamic acid isomers; others, although not identified completely, gave spectra which were almost certainly indicative of higher homologues of cinnamic esters. Such components might well be anticipated to result from compounds to be found among resin products from the Styracaceae and, possibly, the Fabaceae. Utilisation of resinous material from the latter botanical subfamily is unlikely, in this instance at least: resins derived from plants of this group, such as *Myroxylon balsamum* (L.) Harms var. *balsamum* (Tolu balsam) and var. *pereira* (Royle) Harms, are brownish in colour and thus probably unsuitable for general use in painting, particularly in a passage of this colour. In fact, the material detected is more likely to derive from *Styrax tonkinensis* (Pierre) Craib ex Hartwich (Siam benzoin), or *Styrax benzoin* Dryander (Sumatra benzoin); of the two, the latter seems more likely in view of its more pronounced content of cinnamic acid and derivative components. Such material would normally be employed in a spirit base. It is not at all likely that a benzoin resin could be incorporated satisfactorily with a drying oil to form a homogeneous medium and, indeed, more than one layer of paint appeared to be sampled. The brown-black shadow paint of the buoy (sample 3) contained heat-bodied walnut oil as principal binder, together with some pine and mastic resins. In the case of the mastic, in addition to the usual moronic acid component, the presence of nor-olean-18-ene components was quite pronounced and may be the result of tarring. Sample 4, mustard-coloured paint, contained walnut oil, a little pine resin and a triterpenoid resin, probably a dammar.

Pictures Cleaned and Restored in the Conservation Department of the National Gallery, October 1994 – September 1995

Bosschaert *Flowers in a Glass Vase* NG 6549

Canaletto Venice: *The Basin of San Marco on Ascension Day* NG 4453

Canaletto *A Regatta on the Grand Canal* NG 4454

Catena *Portrait of a Young Man* NG 1121

Cavalori *A Discussion* NG 3941

Cranach *Portrait of Johann the Steadfast* NG 6538

Cranach *Portrait of Johann Friedrich the Magnanimous* NG 6539

Gainsborough *Portrait of the Artist with his Wife and Daughter* NG 6547

Girolamo da Carpi *The Adoration of the Kings* NG 640

Gossaert *Man with a Rosary* NG 656

Filippino **Lippi** *The Virgin and Child with Saint John* NG 1412

After **Michelangelo** *The Dream* NG 8

Montagna *The Virgin and Child* NG 1098

Neapolitan School *The Adoration of the Shepherds* NG 232

Poussin *Sleeping Nymph surprised by Satyrs* NG 91